Music in the Market

Music in the Market

Don Cusic

Bowling Green State University Popular Press
Bowling Green, OH 43403

Other books by Don Cusic

Cowboys and the Wild West:
An A-Z Guide from the Chisholm Trail to the Silver Screen

The Poet as Performer

Randy Travis: King of the New Country Traditionalists

Reba: Country Music's Queen

Sandi Patti: The Voice of Gospel

The Sound of Light: A History of Gospel Music

As editor:

Willie Nelson: Lyrics 1957-1994

Hank Williams: The Complete Lyrics

Library of Congress Cataloging-in-Publication Data
Cusic, Don.
Music in the market / Don Cusic.
p. cm.
Includes bibliographical references (p.) and index.
ISBN 0-87972-693-8 (clothbound). -- ISBN 0-87972-694-6 (pbk.)
1. Music trade. 2. Popular music--Economic aspects. I. Title.
ML3790.C87 1996
338.4'778'0973--dc20 95-47158
CIP
MN

Contents

	Acknowledgments	vii
	Introduction	1
1.	Music and Popular Culture	5
2.	Watching the Money Flow	21
3.	Artists and Management	31
4.	The Record Label	41
5.	Retailers and Record Companies	63
6.	Radio and Record Labels	73
7.	Publicity and Advertising in the Media	93
8.	Independent Labels and Specialty Music	117
9.	Technology, Special Marketing, and Discography	149
	Conclusion	169
	Appendix	173
	Selected Bibliography	181
	Index	185

Acknowledgments

For thirteen years I have taught the course "Marketing Recordings" so I must first thank my students for being part of a research laboratory as this book unfolded from lecture notes to this final form. Along the way I received help and input from executives in the music business, especially Dan Beck, Howard Bloom, Jimmy Bowen, Stan Byrd, Jim Foglesong, Joe Galante, Billy Ray Hearn, Lon Helton, Donna Hilley, Bruce Hinton, Nick Hunter, Bill Ivey, Frances Preston, Bob Saporiti, Evelyn Shriver, Lynn Shults, Liz Theils, Dave Wheeler, Roy Wunsch, and numerous others. The time I spent as country music editor of *Record World* (1974–76) and of *Cashbox* (1980–81) were invaluable, because I was able to interview a number of top executives and cover the music business in the role of a journalist with a trade magazine.

Perhaps the most valuable sources for this book are the trade magazines, especially *Billboard*, but also *Radio and Records*. If you read these trades week in and week out, you are sure to get a good, firm grasp on the *business* of music. The insights in the *cultural* aspects of marketing have come from the people I've met at the annual Popular Culture Association meetings, especially Ray and Pat Browne, the great gurus of the popular culture movement in academe.

It is difficult to find good books on this topic because most books about the music business are written from the point of view of the artist trying to break into the business. However, I have included a brief bibliography of some helpful books for further study into this field.

I would like to thank the people I work with at Belmont University, Bob Mulloy, Cliff Eubanks, Larry Wacholtz, James Elliott, Pam Browne, Bill Troutt, and Clyde Rolston and my former cohorts at Middle Tennessee State University, Geoff Hull, Rich Barnet, and Tom Hutchison for their input, encouragement and support. I would like to thank the students in my marketing classes at Belmont and Middle Tennessee State University for serving as workshops for this book, pointing out shortcomings as well as strengths. Their input has been invaluable and appreciated.

Finally, I would like to thank my wife, Jackie, and children Delaney, Jesse, Eli, and Alex for taking my mind off work. I am indebted to the baseball teams of the Crieve Hall league that my sons have played on and which have allowed me to coach.

Introduction

Great music will raise the spirit, move the heart and touch the soul. We all love to hear great music, and experience the effect it can have on us. We like to hear this great music on the radio and on television, we want to read about the artists who bring us this music, and we want to be able to buy this music so we can play it anytime we wish. But while we love the idea of owning and hearing great music, the notion that business and marketing play a part in getting it to our homes sometimes seems to turn us off. Somehow we tend to rebel at the concept of mixing art and business. Yet, they must be mixed for music to thrive in the marketplace and continue to be produced.

For people who love music but are outside the music industry, complaints are often raised about its being called a "product," that big impersonal corporations filled with people dressed in gray with musical tastes to match call the shots, and that somehow the pop charts don't really reflect the music that is the most significant, important, meaningful or influential. Somehow the music industry manages to get the music we love into our homes and onto our stereos, but along the way the marketing machinery appears to strip the music of its very life and soul.

But we cannot study popular music without looking at the capitalist market economy because it is the market that defines and determines what is popular music. No study of artists, recordings, songs or anything else connected with popular music can be complete without taking into account the marketing which delivers these artists, recordings and songs to the public. The technology and the business of the music industry are as important as the artists, recordings or songs because there is a symbiotic relationship between all of these forces.

In many ways the artist shapes the market but in other ways it is the other way around. Certainly no artists without audiences to buy their recordings or attend their concerts will have any lasting impact on popular culture. And the technology is necessary in order for audiences to see and hear an artist. In fact, more people will hear an artist over the electronic medium that will ever see the act in person; also, artists are heavily dependent upon recordings to ensure their legacy, document their career, and preserve their art. And these recordings are done by recording labels—primarily major multinational corporations—who do them because they believe in the profit motive. In short, artists are recorded because it is believed their recordings will sell and generate money for a company. Consumers buy recordings because the artist or song touches them in some way so they want to "own" this recording. Although consumers often disregard or ignore the profit motive while purchasing recordings—sometimes even disparage it or deem it distasteful or irrelevant—the fact remains that these same consumers are an integral part of the capitalist market system.

Whenever artists sign with a recording label they agree to become part of this marketing process. Their music must appeal to an audience somewhere if they are to continue making recordings and be successful at what they do. Also, the artists must be part of the processes of marketing, publicity, and promotion if they are recording with a major label. A major label is a multinational corporation engaged in the business of manufacturing and selling recordings; there are six major labels and they dominate the music industry.

In the end, music may be in the heart, the spirit, and the soul—and that is where it should be. Great music always transcends the daily life of this world. But in American popular culture, the journey to an individual's spirit, heart, and soul must go through the market. And it is music in the market that must be studied if music in the culture is to be understood.

1

Music and Popular Culture

Popular culture is the product of a capitalist, open-market economic system. Rather than a culture that is imposed on a populace from above, popular culture is a culture "chosen" by the populace primarily through economic purchases. Although there may be exceptions (TV shows are viewed and "events" are often free), the link with a capitalist open-market system is always the thread that ties popular culture. This is certainly true in music where the most "popular" music is the music that is purchased by most consumers. Or at least is purchased by a significant number of consumers.

Popular culture is mass culture and popular music is mass music or music that appeals to large numbers of people. Critics of popular culture or mass consumerism often deride popular music because it may not be the "best" or most aesthetically pleasing music, by exacting standards, and because it appeals to the lowest possible denominator, the most common of tastes. But advocates argue that there is a wisdom in the masses, that huge numbers of people somehow know what is "good" and that there is an intrinsic quality and value that appeals to the average person which escapes cultural critics, who may argue that a small group possessing superior knowledge and tastes—cultivated and refined—should define what is best in culture and music. The mass audience argues that cultural critics are in touch only with themselves and, consequently, out of touch with everyday life. While this argument could go on endlessly with each side scoring points in turn, the simple fact remains that popular culture dominates the United States because this country has an open market capitalist economy whereby the most popular entertainment is the most profitable, thus ensuring that entrepreneurs and consumers—as well as business people and entertainers—join forces to give the folks what they want, evidenced by what they buy.

Mass marketing developed in the United States around the turn of the century. Prior to this period, goods were locally made, but by the turn of the century the country was linked by railroad and the telegraph, making it possible for transportation and communication on a national scale. The industrial revolution spurred the creation of mass production through technological advances, and the development of electricity led to further inventions of electrical machines, which further increased mass production capabilities. With the development of mass production came the need for mass marketing in order to sell the goods produced. The recording industry came along as the United States was developing this mass market and benefited from these developments.

When Edison invented the phonograph in 1877 there was no mass market for his machine or early recordings; they appealed primarily to store owners who wanted to attract a crowd. The first commercial phonograph recordings were marketed in 1889 and that market grew steadily through the end of the nineteenth century. But it was Victor Records, which came out of Eldridge Johnson's factory in Camden, New Jersey, that made the gramophone, using Emile Berliner's technological development of the disc, and created the mass market for recordings. Between 1900 and 1910 the disc replaced the cylinder in sales (although the cylinder continued to be produced and marketed until the mid-1920s), while the emergence of

Enrico Caruso as the first international recording "star" created a national demand for his product.

Victor and Columbia continued to develop their machines and the mass market until World War I, which slowed down the recording industry for a few years as factory production shifted to wartime goods. The recording industry made huge gains during the 1920s—a period that corresponds to the institution of the mass market. It also corresponds to the development of radio, which played a major role in the United States becoming a mass market, linked by an entertainment medium.

With the rise of the mass market came the development of a mass culture. The development of national entertainment mediums—radio and movies—created a popular culture dominated by popular entertainment geared to the mass market. The recording industry benefited from these trends, presenting artists of national stature, and marketing recordings all over the country. Indeed, the measure of success for recording artists depended upon their success on a national, rather than a local, scale, and artistic criteria were linked with the potential for mass appeal in the recording company's decision on whether to record an artist. Thus the rise of popular culture came from the development of the mass market and was led by the entertainment industry. The recording industry was part of this creation of a national culture, and it developed with radio and the movies to provide the United States with a popular culture based on mass consumption through the world of entertainment presented in a market-based economy.

Popular Music in Popular Culture

In order to begin to understand the popular music industry, it is necessary to see it as part of the larger popular culture. Popular music does not exist in isolation—it is part of the same culture that creates trends in fashion, promotes fads, encourages lifestyles, and sees buying habits for other types of entertainment, as well as the purchase of electronic equipment, computers, televisions, video cassette recorders and other carriers of this culture, as reflective of this same culture.

Popular culture includes television shows, movies, books, shopping malls, garage sales, concerts, religion, jewelry, amusement parks, celebrities, language, periodicals, food, hobbies, home decorating, automobiles, leisure activities, clothing, hairstyles, material possessions, slang terms, dancing, and a plethora of other things. And the music industry is one of the most important parts of popular culture because it is not only a leader, creating celebrities and role models, fashion trends and slang terms but also a huge business/entertainment complex. Music is social—we listen to it with others and, in selecting our music, we are also picking our friends and being "acceptable" to them. It is also solitary, keeping us company when no one else is around. It is highly individualistic, because we find tunes, phrases, performers, songs, messages, and fashions in music that make deep impressions within us and influence what we do, say, think, feel, and wear. In many ways music connects us to others at the same time it isolates us, reinforcing our individuality at the same time it connects us to a group of like-minded people.

To look at the marketing of music, we must look at it in context. Since music is marketed in the context of popular culture, we must use other elements in popular culture in the marketing process. If this sounds manipulative, it is. But part of marketing is manipulating. The idea of a totally "free" market is misleading; marketers work hard to make sure it is not "free" or "open." Instead, the market is a collection of competing marketers who attempt to capture and control the market through their efforts at mass marketing. The recording industry is part of all this as marketing executives at recording companies work hard to get their product exposed and sold in the marketplace. In a market filled with products that are roughly equal, it is often the product with the best marketing that wins. Marketing alone will not create successful products, nor will an inferior product continually outperform one that is superior. But an understanding of marketing is essential to understand why one product is successful while a competitor falls by the way. Two of the maxims in the recording industry are that you cannot "buy" a hit and you cannot "create" a star; ultimately the consumer decides these questions. But the marketing department can provide ways for consumers to hear recordings, some of which may become hits, and be exposed to artists, some of whom may become stars through acceptance at the consumer level and popularity with listeners.

There are artists who rebel against all this, who insist they will not be part of this whole idea of marketing "product" because their music is too personal and too meaningful for them and those around them. Some of these artists will establish whole new trends, introduce life-changing ideas into the music industry and the popular culture, and become major artists from the stands they take. Ironically, these artists may become the trendsetters whose careers often establish future trends in the marketing of music.

No really successful artist will be totally manipulated and no successful marketing executive will believe that either the artists or the market can be manipulated to suit particular whims or current releases. But both artists and marketers must have an *awareness* of the market and know the tools to reach the people they want to reach. This means being in tune with popular culture, with what people are doing and the trends in the culture. It means being aware of the ways music is marketed. It means marketing managers must know they are selling feelings, emotions, and art as well as "product," and it means that artists must know the necessity of business strategy and tactics in order for their music to be heard. Indeed, a major reason for such a thriving popular culture is that business people have done so well marketing ideas, trends, food, clothing, and other material possessions to perpetuate this culture.

Music in the Market

In order for American popular music to survive in the market it must be commercial. In other words, music must not only inspire people in ways that touch hearts, souls, minds, and spirits, but it must also touch the pockets that carry the means to purchase this music. The true test of music in a capitalist economy is whether it inspires people to part with their money in order to purchase it. If it can do this in great numbers, it is "popular music."

In order for music to succeed in the marketplace it must accept some basic ground rules: (1) music must appeal to consumers who listen to the electronic media; (2) music must appeal to consumers who purchase it; and (3) artists must appeal to consumers so that tickets to concerts and other personal appearances will be sold. If these three basic criteria are met, then music is commercial. Further, for music to be commercial, it must join forces with business and technology in order to reach consumers so it can be heard and purchased.

Since the record labels dominate the music industry—due to the fact they provide the vehicle (recordings) that gives artists exposure—let us first look at the role of the record company. It is *to manufacture, distribute, promote, and sell recordings*. The key word here is *sell*. By and large, major record labels make their decisions about who to sign, how to promote and other marketing decisions with one criterion in mind: will it sell to consumers at the retail level? Lest you think this is totally crass, consider this: The major labels know something very, very important: *it is great music that sells.* Therefore, they want to release and promote great music. But they also have to be cognizant of other considerations along the way.

Record labels only make money when a record or tape or compact disc is sold. They do not make money from radio airplay (that goes to songwriters and publishers), from a successful concert tour (that goes to artists and promoters), or from any source other than a consumer walking into a store and purchasing an album or single. (There are some minor exceptions here: they may lease recordings to TV packagers and others for compilation albums and they may license recordings for movie soundtracks and commercials.)

These huge companies have huge overheads, so they must generate lots of money each and every day if they are to keep their doors open. That means they must *market* music, which inevitably means marketing a wide variety of music for a wide variety of tastes. In a pluralistic society such as that of the United States, there is a wide range of audiences and there will be pockets of mass appeal. Often there will be superstars in some area of music whom fans of other types of music may never have heard of.

These companies operate under the ground rule that only approximately 20 percent of all their album releases will break even financially and that only 5 percent of all their releases will make enough money to allow them to release albums on the other 95 percent of the label's roster. It is a high risk/high payoff business and a first album by a new act is always considered a great risk.

Music recordings are sold primarily in either record stores, like those in free-standing locations or in malls, and in mass merchandisers, such as Wal-Mart, Kmart and Target. A significant number are sold through direct mail, via record clubs, and through direct marketing via television as well.

The primary exposure for music is the radio; studies have consistently shown that the people who buy the most recordings listen to the most radio. Radio serves to introduce new recordings to the public as well as provide established artists to listeners. It is the most pervasive medium; people can listen to the radio in the car, while jogging, at home or in the office. Television, primarily through music videos, is another important outlet for musical acts. Print media is also important for musical acts, providing more in-depth information and news about acts but its prime drawback is that people cannot *hear* acts.

The electronic media are primarily responsible for exposing music and this exposure leads to sales in retail outlets. This, in a nutshell, is how the music industry generally functions: the record label releases a recording, the consumer hears it through the electronic media, which inspires him/her to purchase it at a retail outlet. But beneath this simplicity is a web of complexity as recordings compete for airplay and shelf space in stores.

Then there are the consumers themselves: Who are they? What do they buy? Although buying trends shift, in the past sales have been dominated by the 10-25 age group, with those aged 25-35 also accounting for significant sales. In the past, those over age 50 have been relatively insignificant or "non-buyers" for prerecorded product. However, because baby boomers have continued to buy recordings as they have gotten older, and because there are fewer youth in the 10-19 demographic, there has been a shift in buying habits. First, those over 45 are becoming increasingly important as prerecorded music buyers (almost 15 percent in 1993) while those aged 10-19 account for many fewer sales than they used to (from over 30 percent in 1989 to about 23 percent in 1993). In terms of numbers, the 20-35 year old group accounts for about 40 percent of all prerecorded music purchases, with the 20-24 group accounting for over 15 percent of the total. If the age group extended from 20 to 40 then almost 53 percent of all purchases of prerecorded music would be accounted for. Significantly, though, if the buying public was divided into five year segments (15-19, 20-24, 25-29 etc.), each group from 15-19 to 30-35 is roughly equal. Then the over-45 group accounts for almost as much as the 20-24 group. So consumers for prerecorded music are spread out fairly evenly across a wide age spectrum. Males tend to purchase slightly more than females—a little over half of all prerecorded product is purchased by males while a little under half is purchased by females. In terms of geographic regions, the South purchases almost a third of all prerecorded product sold while the Northeast and West each account for a little over 21 percent (1993 figures).

Musically, we are a diverse nation with the category "rock" accounting for the majority of sales. Other music, such as country and rhythm and blues also have large shares of the audience while music such as classical, gospel, children's and jazz have significant, though much smaller, shares of the market. Generally, record stores sell more rock product with mass merchandisers selling more country and children's product. Independent stores sell the bulk of classical, jazz and other specialty product while Christian book stores sell most gospel product.

There are six major recording labels that dominate the music industry: BMG/RCA, Sony, MCA, WEA, Capitol/EMI, and Polygram. These six multinational corporations (and their subsidiaries) account for about 80 percent of the record sales in this country. The other 20 percent come from small or "independent" labels.

The Business Structure and Popular Music

During the 1980s the theory was promulgated that small businesses created most of the jobs in the American economy, and that small business was the key to innovation in this country. This idea fell on fertile ground and we all wanted to believe it; somehow the idea that gigantic multinational corporations are controlling our lives is not terribly appealing. And the ideas that big business is a dinosaur, that small is beautiful, and that an individual with guts and determination can roll up his or her sleeves and make a difference in the business world is part of the American belief in the free enterprise system. Indeed, the success of individuals and small businesses that grow to become large businesses is an important part of the business history of the United States; it is also part of the intrinsic values of American culture where the cultural climate is such that these things can happen.

Although there are a number of examples of this idea of small businesses providing the backbone for American business, the plain fact is that we are, to a large extent, ruled by big business. This is especially true in the music industry where the six multinational recording corporations dominate the global and domestic mainstream commercial music business. These six multinationals account for approximately 80-85 percent of the revenues generated by the sale of recordings in the United States.

These large firms form a number of networks, deals, and alliances in the technology, finance, and distribution—as well as alliances with governments—in their daily business. Smaller firms, especially those in the fields of publishing, management, booking, public relations, independent promotion, production companies and studios, tend to act as the followers and suppliers of these large firms, heavily dependent upon the success of these large firms for their own survival.

As an example, let us look at the career of a recording artist. First, the act will develop their talents in small clubs or other venues—all small businesses—and perhaps be signed by a manager who will work to put together a team for this act. This "team" may consist of a music publisher, a publicist, a booking agency and others who are all part of small businesses. But the success of this act on a national scale depends upon their being signed by one of the six major labels. At this point all of the small businesses involved with the act function as a *supplier* to this large corporation.

At the large corporation the act has access to large sums of money not available to small businesses in order to produce a studio recording, produce a video, and get these recordings and videos distributed nationally into record stores and onto radio stations and TV stations. A record store may be owned by an individual (although they are increasingly chain owned) or the radio station may be essentially a "small" business, but they are dependent on this large multinational corporation to supply them with the artist's recordings.

Meanwhile, the management company, publishing company, publicity company, booking agency, and others associated with the artist are now dependent upon the major label for their own growth; even though these companies connected to the artist may be small businesses—and play a vital, important role in this process—their success is tied directly to the success of the major label in exposing and marketing this artist.

This example may be continued and enlarged but the point has been made; it is the major recording labels who generally control the destinies of the myriad small companies that constitute the music business. Although these major labels may have a smaller number of people employed than all the others combined, the employment practices of these small business are dependent upon the activities of this large corporation. Thus while small businesses are vital and important, the mainstream commercial music industry is, in fact, guided and controlled by the dominant multinational corporations.

At this point it should be pointed out that the recording labels are not the only large multinational corporations in the music industry. Booking agencies, publishing companies, and management firms may also be large multinationals. All of these large corporations are dependent upon small businesses as suppliers, and these small businesses are in turn heavily dependent on the large multinationals for their own existence and growth. Too, successful large corporations have learned that breaking themselves up into smaller groups or "businesses" under the large corporate umbrella fosters the creativity and dynamism of the small business mentality in a multinational firm. The recording industry has done this by creating small labels with small rosters of artists under the large corporate umbrella, where the advantages of the big company's sales force and distribution system can be combined with the small company's advantages of close contact with artists and the creative process to get the best of both worlds.

Having said that, it is now time to present another idea: small, independent recording labels dominate the music industry in the nonmainstream music field. Indeed, small labels often provide the creative backbone for the recording industry; new musical trends and new artists are often discovered and first recorded by small "indies," as they are called. In this sense, small businesses *are* the key to innovation to the recording industry. Too, these small labels provide an alternative to the mainstream commercial music industry, providing music the major labels do not market because the market is not large enough. Sometimes, in the case of rap or dance music, the music does enter the mainstream, at which time the major labels step in and take over the marketing and distribution, signing the acts to major label contracts.

In summary, the mainstream commercial recording industry is dominated by six multinational corporations, the major recording labels; their success is the engine that makes the recording industry a thriving, global industry. However, small businesses are essential to these major labels as suppliers of talent and other services. At the same time, small independent recording labels dominant the non-mainstream music in the recording industry. Further, these small labels often discover new talent and new musical trends before the major labels are even aware of them; in this sense, the independents are essential to the creative side of the music industry. And though these small indies only account for 15-20 percent of the recording industry, for an industry that generates approximately $12 billion annually, 15-20 percent is a significant amount of money.

Marketing Music

Like most other businesses in the entertainment industry, marketing in the music industry is guided by the general notion that entertainment marketing should be aimed toward the youth market. TV and radio advertisers demand programs that reach the young (10-24) demographic. The reasoning is that (1) young people, although they have fewer disposable dollars and smaller gross incomes than those over 45, are more active shoppers and spenders and that (2) the older, adult audiences tend to buy successful youth-oriented products because they like the appeal of youth-oriented product. In other words, people over 25—even when they're over 45—like the self-image of youth as well as the idea of feeling young.

The youth market—generally considered the 13-25 demographic—is, in terms of percentages, a relatively small part of the population (always less than half) but their influence extends beyond these numbers to the "youth-oriented" or "youth-conscious" adult market. When questioned about an ideal age ("If you could be any age at all, how old would you be?"), individuals generally chose the early to mid-twenties. This is because people want to be vigorous and energetic, vital, strong, and aware, and keep abreast of youthful trends. In a sense, entertainment marketing is geared to this "ideal age."

In looking at the 13-25 demographic, three distinct groups emerge: teenagers, noncollege young adults, and young adults in college. This youth market has a large amount of discretionary dollars to spend. Furthermore, this group also wields enormous power to influence the larger, adult markets.

These young people are important consumers because they are just beginning to develop loyalties to particular brands and are more likely to try something new and different. In fact, teenagers determine the purchase of products such as records, shoes, stationery and school supplies, jewelry, radios, snack foods, health and beauty aids, sporting equipment, and movies. They also choose the stores where the purchases are made. Older consumers, on the other hand, are more likely to spend discretionary dollars on big-ticket items and less likely to be active, engaged shoppers.

In marketing to youth, it is important to know the youth mind-set. This includes what young people talk about, how they view their friends and parents, what they like to buy, what they don't like and how they hope the rest of the world will treat them or perceive them. Basically, these people need to be "different" yet fit in with certain groups; need to appear independent to their friends yet feel loved by their parents; need to complain about their parents and rebel against institutions and need to create a public image for themselves.

This need to be different means they don't want to be like their parents or their ruling institutions. They want the chance to say no, to reject the direction of elders, to feel in control of their lives. Generally, the things they can control are their language, their clothing, and their entertainment.

We have two forces pulling on us: the need to feel as individuals and the need to feel part of a group. Young people want to belong to some group, do not want to feel alone. For this reason, the strongest forces acting on junior high and high school students is peer pressure; this is manifested as they adapt tastes in clothing, language, and music of their peers.

Perhaps the overriding feeling of junior high and high school students is one of rebellion. This rebellion is a way of asserting individuality, or separating their identity from that of their parents and establishing their own individual identity, reinforced by their friends and peers. This rebellion expresses itself by opposition to authority figures, including parents, as well as the norms and values of people who are older or society in general. This idea of resisting authority makes young people feel more daring and independent. Often this is expressed in their musical tastes. In fact, the music of choice in young people is generally rock, but if you attempt to define all the music labeled under the category of "rock" you will find a wide variety of music. That is because "rock" is not a style of music; it is an attitude. And that attitude can be summed up briefly as "rebellion."

In marketing products to the youth culture, the entertainment industry often caters to this theme of rebellion. And the entertainment industry picks up on ideas and turns them into fads and trends quicker than any other kinds of business. This entertainment industry is usually willing to gamble on offering unique products, and campaigns that shock. They are willing to puzzle, excite, or annoy consumers because they are confident consumers will buy. This all begins by targeting the youthful consumer who wants to rebel against the status quo through music and other forms of entertainment.

In order to understand how and why consumers buy music recordings, let us look at the internal structure of the music industry to see how it functions and how it delivers music in the market.

Although some may view the music industry as soulless, stifling, arbitrary, and chaotic, there are methods to the madness. There are tried and proven ways of getting exposure for artists and recordings, of getting recordings to consumers, and of convincing consumers and the media that the label has a viable product.

2

Watching the Money Flow

In discussing the music industry, one of the first questions asked is, "Where does the money come from?" This question is generally followed by "How is it generated?" "Who gets the money?" and "How do they get it?"

Since artists are the most visible part of the music industry, and serve as a central focus for the generation of information about the industry, they can serve as the key factor in the discussion of money—a successful act is the major source of money in the music industry. To discuss how the artist generates money for the industry, let us look first at the three basic ways a consumer becomes aware of an artist. These avenues of consumer awareness are also the three basic ways an artist generates money: through performances in the electronic media, through personal appearances, and from sales of recordings.

People hear an artist through a recording played on radio, a performance on video, or on television. Each radio station and each television station pays a *performance rights organization* (PRO), such as ASCAP, BMI, or SESAC, a certain amount of money—generally based on ratings, income, size of market, and some other factors—in order to have the right to play an artist's recordings. The PROs provide broadcasters a *license* to play recordings, thus assuring the industry it will be paid for its work. Actually, these agreements between the performing rights organization and broadcast stations do not occur on an artist-by-artist (or song-by-song) basis but are structured through "blanket license" agreements. This means that each station will pay BMI one sum for the right to play any song licensed by BMI and another amount to ASCAP for the right to play any song licensed by ASCAP. Since all songs must be licensed for airplay, these performance licenses generate the income from airplay for all songs.

The money received from airplay (performances) goes to songwriters and publishers. Neither the artist nor the record company receives any money from exposure on radio or a television broadcast of a song or performance. (The artist may receive money from a personal appearance on TV but not from a songs being played.) The money flow goes from the station to the performing rights organization to the songwriters and publishers. The performance rights organizations determine how much each song earns from randomly sampling stations across the country, then using a formula to determine how much airplay the song is receiving nationally. This formula works much like public opinion polls where a small sample generates data that can be used to summarize how the whole country feels about a given issue, candidate, or subject. The exception is SESAC, which uses SoundScan, a technology that samples all the songs being played on a group of stations and bases its payments on a wider sample.

The generation of "performance monies" benefits the publishing side of the music industry. The money generated from "performances," both broadcast and nonbroadcast, is one of the two major sources of revenue for songwriters and publishers. (Clubs, halls, and other venues with live music must pay a fee to the performing rights organizations for the privilege of playing music publicly; the PROs then disperse this money to songwriters and publishers.) The other major source is money generated from the sales of recordings is called "mechanicals" because the original provision for this income came from the 1909 Copyright Act that was aimed at player pianos whose "mechanical" reproductions provided the legal base for copyright protection for the recording industry. The recording industry did not have the power or prestige to exert influence on this 1909 law at the time it was written.

Other sources of publishing revenue are generated by licenses or permits to use the copyright. Licenses are provided to sheet music publishers, those using songs in broadcast commercials or theatrical productions, cable TV, movies, jukeboxes, recordings in foreign countries, and other ancillary uses of music (talking dolls, music boxes, etc.) in exchange for either a flat fee or a royalty.

These examples show the importance of copyrights in the music industry. Understanding copyrights and copyright law is essential to understand the recording industry.

Each song is copyrighted by a publisher, which means the publisher and *not* the songwriter owns the song. Whoever owns the song can control its use and receive a financial benefit when it is used. There is also a form of copyright used for recorded product so that recording companies *own* the recordings produced for their label and therefore control the uses of these recordings and receive financial remuneration when recordings are used for ancillary purposes, such as in broadcast commercials or in movies.

The consumer, of course, does not pay directly for hearing a song on radio or television. Broadcast stations receive their income from advertising, and the price of consumer products includes advertising costs. Thus consumers pay indirectly—through higher prices for advertised products in stores—in order to hear their favorite artists on radio and television. Broadcasters benefit because with the audience they have attracted they sell time to advertisers who want to reach this audience. Artists benefit because they receive exposure, which leads to other opportunities for income.

A second way consumers hear artists is through personal appearances. Here, the consumer pays directly, putting down money in order to buy a ticket to a club or concert where the artist is performing. The cash flow goes from the consumer to the promoter of the show to the booking agent and the artist. The artist will benefit directly from personal appearances, receiving either a flat fee or some combination of guaranteed fee and percentage of the gross receipts for attracting an audience. The record company does not receive any money from personal appearances by an act.

The act, on the other hand, receives most of their income from live appearances. In real terms, artists make no money from publishing or songwriting if they don't write; if they do write and have a hit, they must wait about a year in order to receive their money from a current hit. Further, only a handful of artists receive money from royalties from the sale of recordings and, again, must wait a year or more to receive this money. But artists are regularly paid for live performances and this is where they generate their day-to-day income.

Artists are booked by *booking agents,* who contract with *promoters* to schedule an artist into a facility, or venue, for either a flat fee, a percentage of the income from ticket sales, or a combination of both (usually a guaranteed fee plus a percentage of the gate). Booking agents generally take a commission from the bookings—usually 10 to 15 percent—and the artist's manager also receives a percentage. For their commission, booking agents spend their days on the phone making calls to promoters and club owners in order to convince them to book the act into their venue. Promoters generally receive their income from the profits of concerts. The promoter is usually an independent business person who will contract for the act, rent a venue, advertise and promote the concert and, hopefully, generate enough ticket sales to receive a profit for the venture.

The third way income is generated in the music industry is through sales of recordings in stores. Again, the consumer pays directly for this, putting down money in order to pay for a recording. The money flow goes from the consumer to the store to the record company, which pays a portion of each sale to the artist via royalty payments (also called artist royalties).

Most of the money generated in the music industry comes through these three major revenue streams: broadcast performances, personal appearances, and sales of recordings. This income supports those involved in the music industry: broadcast personnel, record store personnel, record companies, publishing companies, songwriters, musicians, publicists, promoters, managers, road crews, and, of course, the artists.

Many people ask about studios and musicians and the money generated there. For commercial recordings, this comes primarily from the record company, which advances the costs of production. Publishing companies also use studios and musicians to "demo" songs by their songwriters. Thus studios and musicians receive money indirectly from the sales of recordings and broadcast performances. Finally, there is the inevitable observation about someone who has worked and saved their money for years in order to finance a recording session. Where does this fit in? Actually, while these efforts are laudable, they are relatively insignificant in discussing the cash flow of the recording industry.

From Song to Stereo

The music industry is fond of saying, "It all begins with a song," and that is where the discussion of "product flow" and the marketing process must begin.

After a songwriter writes a song, it then goes to a studio where it is recorded by the artist and producer, mixed to a two-track tape, and sent to the manufacturer. The manufacturer usually releases a cassette and compact disc into the distribution network, which gets the product into record retailers. These retailers make it available for consumers to purchase, which is the only way the record company receives income.

The company also sends the recording to selected media, because media exposure is essential for consumers to become aware of songs, albums, and acts. Usually, this involves getting a single played on the radio, getting exposure on television through appearances on regularly scheduled shows or "specials" and video clips, and getting written up in the print media. Exposure in the media leads to consumer awareness, which, hopefully, leads to consumer purchases. This, in a nutshell, is the marketing process and product flow for recordings released by a recording label.

Marketing

The record company's marketing department is where the strategy for selling recordings is developed. The day-to-day function of the marketing department involves creating, implementing, coordinating, and directing efforts and activities in advertising, publicity, promotion, and selling recordings. Factors to consider when developing a strategy to market an act include (1) what other recordings the label is releasing; (2) what other product is in the marketplace (from other labels as well as the home label); (3) the act's past success or failure; (4) the contractual commitments of the label to the act; (5) subjective considerations about the potential for major success for the act; (6) and numerous other factors that range from personalities to financial statements.

The marketing department coordinates the activities of promotion, publicity, sales, and advertising. It will take the finished product—after the studio production is finished and the cover art has been decided—and try to develop a plan for maximum exposure for the act. If the act is "new" the marketing department will probably not want to commit much money until the product has received some kind of positive acceptance, generally on radio. The company will then seek ways to convince consumers to buy the product. Other tests for the product include concert tours, videos, success in a particular market (perhaps a city or region), print stories, TV or movie exposure, or other name recognition of the act.

For a major act with a lot of past success, the label will probably have a marketing plan developed before the single or album is released. Changes in this plan, or perhaps more plans, will be developed depending upon the success or failure of the single and album to generate airplay and sales in the early stages of its release.

Marketing oversees the spending of money by a label. As a general rule, every dollar spent should generate an album sale. The purpose of spending money is to make consumers aware of an act and an album. This coincides with the primary role of the recording company: *To make the product available at the retail level so that consumers have the opportunity to purchase it*. Therefore, it is important that a label not only get the recordings played on the radio, stories printed in newspapers and periodicals, and other activities that make consumers aware of an act and an album, but that the albums be distributed effectively so they can be purchased by consumers.

The Media Layer

Between the recording label and the consumers is the media layer. It is the media—radio, television, and print—

that is the crucial bridge between recordings and consumers. In order for consumers to know about acts, albums, and songs, the label must somehow find a way to receive exposure through the media. This is done in three ways: radio promotion, publicity, and advertising.

Radio promotion involves getting records played on radio stations and is handled by the promotion department at a record label. Time buys (advertisements) on radio stations are generally handled by the advertising department under the direction of the marketing department. The advertising department, under the direction of the marketing department, also handles time buys on television and ad purchases in print. The publicity department handles exposure on television and print that is part of regular programming or editorial. In this sense it is "free," which means the exposure is not purchased. Exposure on television can be through talk shows, specials, variety shows, and so forth—or on video clips. Exposure in print can mean articles and photos in local media such as newspapers, the trade press, the music press, and general interest publications. This will be discussed in more depth in chapter 7 on "Publicity."

Why People Buy Recordings

There are five major reasons people buy recordings. The buyer may (1) hear the recording and like it; (2) see the act and like them; (3) be a fan of the act; (4) purchase as a gift; (5) be impelled by word of mouth.

The first reason, "hear the recording and like it," is the most common way people decide they want to own some prerecorded product. Usually a song, or single, is heard on the radio, and the appeal of this song causes consumers to buy the album that contains this song. The second reason, "see the act" may occur through television and video (although acts are also "heard" too) or at a personal appearance of the act. While seeing and hearing are obviously linked, they are also two different appeals; when a song is heard, the consumer does not know what the act looks like and bases a decision on sound. But when an act is seen, the appearance of the act is at least as important as the music they play. Concerts are social events and people often go to concerts without having purchased a recording of the act performing. These consumers may be persuaded to purchase a recording of the act if they enjoy the concert, if they are impressed with the act's performance, or if they hear songs they like—perhaps songs previously heard on the radio.

Some acts have developed dedicated audiences, "fans of the act," from their previous successful songs and albums or even from strong personal appearances and touring. These acts have a following that will purchase a new album as soon as it is released, without even hearing it. For a recording company, this is important because it guarantees the company a certain number of sales as soon as the recording is released with virtually no effort in marketing other than making core fans aware a new album is out. Name recognition of the act is insured, so that critical element in marketing has been met that allows the label to pursue sales beyond the initial number sold on release. This appeal is certainly not eternal—the popularity of top acts always comes to an end—but it certainly provides a nice point in the career of an act because they do not have to depend so heavily on a hit single to sell albums.

The fourth reason people buy albums, "as a gift," means people will buy an album they do not particularly like or care for—but which someone else does. For example, on birthdays and especially Christmas, parents and relatives often purchase recordings for their children. This factor is especially significant during December when approximately 50 percent of all albums purchased are gifts.

Sales from the fifth reason for purchase, "word of mouth," may occur when a close and trusted friend with shared taste in music recommends a particular recording or act. It is also part of peer pressure and peer approval—especially among young people—to buy an album recommended by those they wish to emulate. This also extends to musicians or "stars" whom consumers admire. When these artists talk about a major influence or their favorite act or album during an interview, the fans of these artists will often buy an album the artist loves or recommends—an example of word of mouth working through the media.

3

Artists and Management

There are ten basic ways in which a recording act can "break," or reach a significant level of recognition and acceptance with the public, identified by the achievement of goals established by a recording company. These goals may include obtaining a certain chart position on the trade charts (i.e. Top 10), the achievement of a predetermined level of sales, and exposure obtained in the mass media. The level of success the company sets for an act in order to "break" will usually be established in the marketing plan; this plan and these goals are usually developed in consultation that label personnel, the artist's manager, booking agent, and others who are involved in the artist's career.

The ten ways or methods by which an act can break are these:

1. *Radio.* This is the most common because the people who buy the most recordings listen to radio. If an act is successful with radio, this will be reflected on the trade charts, which list the most popular recordings in descending order and indicate a consumer awareness. The method generally used for an act to break on radio is through the label's promotion department getting a single to radio stations and convincing programmers to play it.

2. *Videos.* With the advent of MTV in 1981, the video market became an important and significant media for the recording industry. Since then, a number of other video outlets have emerged. As in radio, exposure on video is

dependent on being played in high rotation (that is, often throughout the day or evening) for maximum exposure and, hopefully, maximum sales. Video has proven to be an alternative to radio in some instances, although the general rule seems to be that a recording must be a hit on radio before the video will generate significant sales. At retail, the major advantage of video is that it gives an artist a visual image and often links for consumers the recording with the name of the act.

3. *Television.* Appearances on a "special," a late-night talk show, or a popular show bring consumer awareness. Appearances on TV, especially a role in a regular series, generate name recognition. If an artist performs a song this will generate interest in the recordings of that act. Performances on awards shows, especially the Grammys, are known to stimulate sales of recordings. A surge in the sales of an artist's recordings is generally experienced for several weeks after one of these performances before a large TV audience. Obviously, these appearances are different from videos, where the artist is presented in a more controlled format.

4. *Personal appearances.* Some acts establish their appeal and create a following through personal appearances. This is particularly true of acts who engage in very theatrical performances (Kiss and Alice Cooper are good examples here) or those who tour incessantly (such as heavy metal acts), or those whose live shows are especially dynamic (such as Bruce Springsteen).

5. *Theater.* Historically, the theater has always played a vital role in American pop music, and the rock world has seen hit songs come out of musicals like *Jesus Christ Superstar, Godspell, Hair* and even *The Sound of Music* and *My Fair Lady*. More recent examples of popular music in theater include *Cats, Les Miserables,* and *Phantom of the Opera*. Although the 1970s and 1980s have seen a decline in

the influence of theater in rock music, there has never been a time when the theater and popular recording industry were not linked in some way. Hit recordings and star performers have often come from musical theater, although in recent history it has been popular music that has influenced musical theater more than the other way around.

6. *Print media.* The print media can play a significant role in informing the public about an act. With exposure in general interest magazines such as *Time* and *Newsweek* combined with exposure in the music press and trade magazines, an act can achieve a significant level of recognition, which will lead to demand for appearances and recordings. The role of the print media tends to emphasize the development of the image of an act, through pictures and interviews, and allows consumers to gain more information about the artist than is generally available in the other media.

7. *In-store airplay.* When consumers are in a record store, they are open to making a purchase and the music played over the store system may influence them. Certain acts as well as certain types of music—jazz, particularly New Age jazz—seem to have an appeal here. Actually, much of New Age jazz's initial exposure came from in-store airplay in bookstores, where it served as good, relaxing background music when book buyers browsed. Later, it received extensive airplay in other types of stores, such as clothing and "nature" stores, in addition to record stores. This in-store airplay is where many consumers were first exposed to New Age jazz.

8. *Movies.* An appearance of an act in a hit movie, or a hit movie soundtrack featuring an act, may play a major role in creating or expanding an audience for an act. It is another way for a consumer to become aware of an act outside the more usual outlets of radio, TV, and print.

9. *Dance clubs.* Beginning with the disco craze, which melted into "dance music" or "dance clubs," a demand developed for recordings that fit the social and cultural atmosphere of dance clubs. Acts that can consistently appeal to this audience through music that inspires dancers to get out on the floor will generate a demand and will have an outlet to be heard in.

Interestingly, country music also has a significant appeal in country dance clubs where, like their pop music counterparts, people want to enjoy a social evening of dancing.

10. *Word of mouth.* Again, this is the most effective way to convince consumers to purchase recordings, and thus for an act to break, but it is also the most difficult to control or create. When a group of people like an act or album, their word-of-mouth communication will create sales. This is particularly true with junior high and high school students where peer pressure is a major determinate for musical tastes and consumer purchases.

The Artist's Team

Breaking an act is a team effort and the marketing department wants to be assured the act has a team in place, or potentially in place, before the act will be signed. Since marketing people are business people involved in the business of marketing a musical act, they feel more comfortable talking business with someone with a business perspective connected to the act. That someone is usually the manager, who is the key figure in pulling the parts of the team together into a cohesive and coherent whole. Further, the team allows the artist to do what an artist does best: record and perform. Obviously, the business aspects of a career must be taken care of in order for an artist to be a commercial success, but the artist should not be concerned with business affairs to the detriment of the job of performing and recording. The key link between the artist and the business of marketing music is the manager.

In addition to a manager, the artist's team will usually be composed of an accountant, an attorney, and a road manager. Each of these may in fact function as a personal manager, and each of these jobs is part of the management function although different people may do them.

The record company brings a number of key players to the artist's team, including a promotion person, publicist, marketing executives, sales people, and the distribution system, which gets the product into the marketplace. In addition, the company name itself provides clout. The booking agent is an integral part of the artist's team because this is the person who books dates that provide the artist with exposure as well as income. If an artist is not performing, an important factor for marketing that act is missing. In addition to bookers, promoters are also necessary because they take the financial risk to have an act perform in a club or concert. It is especially important that some promoters believe in a new artist enough to take this risk and give the artist an opportunity to perform during a critical part of a career before the artist has achieved hit records or national recognition.

In addition to the promotion people and publicists with the record label, the artist may also have an independent promotion person and an independent publicist working as part of their team. Before the label signs an act, the independent publicity people may be the key links between the artist and the media and may actually play a key role in getting a major label to take notice of the act.

A link with a publisher is also essential for an artist because it ensures a source of material or, if the artist is a songwriter, that the copyrights will be fully exploited, thus ensuring additional exposure as well as income for the act. Too, it is essential that all the paperwork and licenses be handled properly when a song is released on recordings; the publisher can do this. Often, the publisher is the key to developing an act through studio recordings of song demos of the act's material as well as perhaps exposing the act to producers looking for talent.

The final key element on the artist's team is the producer. This is the person who gets the artist on tape in the studio, finding songs as well as musicians who will bring out the best in the act. The producer must create a recording atmosphere that allows the artist to be comfortable and do their best. Additionally, the producer must have a good ear for a commercial song, the technical competence to produce a commercial recording, and the musical taste to communicate with musicians, as well as the business acumen to communicate with marketing executives at a record company.

Management

There are five attributes of great musical artists: (1) talent, (2) charisma, (3) competitiveness, (4) burning desire to perform live, and (5) a certain uniqueness.

This quality of talent can be deceptive, although it is certainly essential and most artists initially come to the attention of others in the music industry and get signed to recording contracts because of their talent. But in the long run, it may be of lesser importance than some of the other attributes, although talent is *always* important. However, talent alone will not get a performer very far—other elements in a person's character, personality, or lifestyle may override the talent. Too, the other four characteristics can become more important than the initial raw talent. Talent alone is not enough in the recording industry; there must be a total commitment to a career to go along with it. And if there is a discrepancy, then the commitment is often more vital than the basic talent in commercial music.

The second criterion is charisma, which is a certain magnetic appeal that attracts people to a performer. In many ways this is an inherent part of a person—either it is there or it isn't—although it can also be developed through clothes, hairstyle, lifestyle, or through an articulate manner in interviews. There is a certain amount of charisma any performer achieves simply by standing in front of a microphone; an audience is generally willing to give a performer the benefit of the doubt at first. But the performer must deliver.

Performers are known to be competitive—with other performers and with themselves. Often, a performer will listen to the radio or the recording of another artist and say, "I could sing that better!" Or they will see someone else in concert and say, "I can put on a better show than that!" In many ways, it is a healthy rivalry, keeping artists striving to better present themselves to their audiences. Artists may also be intensely competitive within themselves—perfectionists who want each song, each recording, each performance, to be better than the last.

Great artists have a burning desire to perform live, to express their talents in front of an audience—no matter if it is a roomful of friends or an auditorium full of strangers. In the music business, this means a performer must absolutely burn for the road. With the advent of video and video-clips, many thought this medium would replace live performances. These visionaries did not know the essence of a great artist, who absolutely needs a live audience. Too, an audience does not go to a concert just to hear and see a mere performance—they go for an *event* and a social occasion. Great performers create great events with their concerts. This, in turn, creates a buzz among those who attend the concert that spreads to those who did not see the event.

The final factor is a certain uniqueness possessed by an artist. Most of the time, this is an unconscious thing, and even artists are often unaware of their own uniqueness. Sometimes it is something they have to say, sometimes it is their background, or their lifestyle, or their humor, or their particular style of singing or playing, which is unique to them alone because of limitations as well as God-given gifts.

Most performers do not possess all of these attributes; those that possess all five are in a special category. But even having all these is not enough because management must also play a key role. Nothing just "happens" and, for a performer and artist, it is the manager who is the instigator, the catalyst, and the visionary who makes the career move forward.

The key element between an artist and a manager is trust. The artist must trust the manager totally with their career and with decisions. Most people are not "manageable" in this sense—they will not trust someone else to make major decisions for them about their life and career and follow those decisions. It takes a very special kind of trust to follow someone else's decision. It is that ability to do what an artist does—record and perform—while letting the manager do what a manager does—manage—that often separates the few top acts from a host of those who never make it to the top.

Managers take care of the myriad details in an artist's life, allowing the artist to be an artist. The most frustrating thing in the world for an artist is having to make daily business decisions, arrange press interviews, answer correspondence, maintain record company relations, stay in contact with concert promoters, and the other things that are necessary to do in order to maintain a successful career. This is the importance of a manager in the life and career of the artist.

Another vital function of the manager is to shield an artist. When a manager makes a decision, everyone cannot be happy. Those who are not happy can always blame the manager—who can be the bad guy—while the artist can remain above the fray. It is convenient for the artist, in awkward situations, to say the manager has made the decision, even when the artist's own input was vital and perhaps decisive. It is a way out for an artist, and an artist needs a way out, a scapegoat, and a protector. It gives an artist a lift to be comfortable knowing that he or she will not be in sticky situations, that all of the details have been taken care of, and that someone is watching out for his or her best interests at all times.

4

The Record Label

The A & R (artists and repertoire) department of a recording label is in charge of finding new talent and signing acts to the label. This department generally has the final say over whether an act will be signed or not, but they do not make their decisions alone. Usually, the marketing department has important input on label signings.

Even though there are people with the recording label who have the power to sign an act without asking anyone else's advice or opinions, they rarely if ever do this. Other departments must also be excited about the act, the label's marketing people must feel they can sell the act, and other opinions and views will give a more balanced view of the act. There may be other motivations too: individual tastes may not be in the mainstream and there is a human need to have others affirm our decisions, but the fact is, signing and marketing an act is a team effort. The publicity people must publicize it, the manager must do his/her job, the sales people must get the product in the marketplace while the A & R people must feel that the act is new, fresh and exciting musically.

The A & R person will first be interested in the act's talent and their music. The A & R department must also ascertain whether the act is able to work well with the label, their source of song material, and whether the act has long-term as well as short-term potential. The marketing department, on the other hand, will look to determine a relationship with the act and the marketplace as well as with the roster currently on the label. First is the question of whether there is a need on the roster for this act. For example, if there are 15 solo female singers and the new act is a female singer, then maybe the label should not sign her. Or perhaps there are only two male solo acts on the label so there is a need for more solo male singers, which puts the label in the position of *seeking* an act like this. The label's roster of acts must be balanced as to makeup (male groups, female groups, male solo, female solo, mixed groups) as well as musically (vocalists, instrumentalists, and encompassing musical diversity as well as the trends on the charts).

Another consideration is audience. Who does this act appeal to? Is there someone on the label already successful in this market? Are there acts on other labels who are reaching a market that this company is not reaching? Is there a market already or will one have to be developed? How can this market be reached?

The roster for a label also needs to be balanced between developing acts, mid-level acts, and superstars. It is not advisable to have a label full of developing acts since these acts do not make money and therefore the label cannot support them. But the label must have some developing acts, because from this group will come tomorrow's superstars. There is a need for some mid-level acts—acts that have an audience and are somewhat successful in the market—because they have the potential to break even bigger. Finally, there is the need for some superstars on the label both for income and to attract promising new acts.

According to recording company figures, only 20 percent of all acts on a label will break even, about 80 percent will lose money, while only the top 5 percent will make enough income through sales to support the entire label. However, when an act is in the top 5 percent, they generally want more money for their success, higher royalty rates, and bigger advances, as well as other demands—so a label must be careful to not only have superstars but have them signed to contracts that are beneficial to the label as well as the stars themselves.

Contracts

After the label has agreed to sign an act, the recording contract is negotiated by the legal department of the label with the artist's attorney. It is not the purpose of this work to delve into the intricacies of a recording contract; they are complicated and contain many details about a label's commitment to the act and vice versa. However, contracts *always* obligate the label to *manufacture, distribute, promote and sell* the recordings while the artist is required to *provide recordings suitable for release.* Beyond this, a number of factors are negotiable, especially with "recoupables" or "charge-backs."

The recording company serves somewhat as a venture capitalist for an act; it advances the act money in order to record the album and engage in special marketing. In return, the act must pay back the label through royalties generated from sales before the act can begin receiving money. The investments the label makes which it recoups are called charge-backs or recoupables. Recoupables include the actual production of the album (studio time, musicians, cost of the engineer), the cost of the producer, and advertisement and marketing beyond the basic amount the label does for any act. For example, the costs incurred for a special marketing campaign where the label runs in-store contests, prints posters and flats for stores, and pays for the artist to visit radio stations and stores may all be charged back to the artist. An important part of contract negotiations involves determining which costs are recoupable and which are not. For example, a superstar act can demand the label run advertisements in the trade magazines when the act's album is released and that this cost is absorbed by the label; a new act, on the other hand, may see these costs charged back to them.

In general, the more a label is required to do at its own expense concerning advertising and promotion, the sooner the act can earn money. Conversely, the more the label charges back to the artist's account, the more sales will be required before an artist will receive any money from artist royalties.

Costs Recoupable and Non-recoupable

Labels consider the costs of mailing promotional copies to radio stations and key print-media personnel, the normal day-to-day activities of publicity, such as sending out press kits and press releases, and the normal activities of promotion, calling radio stations, to be part of their operating budget. As such they are not charged against an artist's account and are non-recoupable. Other non-recoupable costs include a minimum amount of advertising, office expenses, manufacturing costs, and sending advance cassettes of the artist's product to the label's in-house personnel.

Recoupable expenses include the studio production of the recordings, videos, tour support, monetary advances in order to help the artist buy equipment or live while a project is being recorded, independent promotion, special promotions, and extensive marketing plans, which may include point-of-purchase (POP) material such as stand-ups, mobiles, and other special displays sent to retailers, special packaging for the product, time buys on radio and television, advertising in the print media, special contests (in-store as well as consumer), talk tours (where an artist visits with key media and retail personnel in various cities), and special showcases where an artist performs for small groups, usually consisting of key media, distributors, and retailers.

In computing costs, a label must take into account fixed costs, semivariable costs and fully variable costs. For example, a label must pay salaries to executives and secretaries, the phone bill, the electric bill, and rent or mortgage payments no matter if an album is released or not. These are fixed costs. Semivariable costs are one-time expenses: the production costs of the album, the design of the album cover, and the initial shipping of the album. Most of these costs are recoupable. Fully variable costs include manufacturing costs (which depend upon the number of albums manufactured), mechanical and other royalties, shipping, and special marketing plans that go beyond the basic day-to-day activities all labels engage in for their artists and products.

Production Costs

The production budget, usually developed by the A & R department, establishes the amount the artist and producer are budgeted to spend in the studio on the production of the recording. While the marketing department is not involved in these costs, it must be aware that there are hourly studio rates for recording and that it may take 100 to 120 hours of recording time and an additional 40 to 60 hours of time for mixing, that there are costs for tape, payments to be made to the unions (AFM for musicians and AFTRA for singers), a producer's fee, and other expenses (such as food during the sessions and other out-of-pocket expenses) as well as some personal advances for the artists as living expenses while the album is being recorded.

Packaging

Packaging is the album's cover art as well as the jewel box for CDs and the plastic case for cassettes. Most labels attempt to charge 10 percent of sales against the artist's account to cover this cost. The reasoning is that the more albums pressed, the more covers and packaging must also be manufactured, so it is an ongoing cost. Some major acts may argue this cost is high and negotiate it lower or eliminate it altogether. However, most acts—especially new acts—have this 10 percent charge leveled against them. Additional allowances may be given for special pressings or half-speed mastering or a special package that contains a cover that opens up or a pop-out or some other extravagant gimmick.

Mechanical Royalties

Record companies must pay mechanical royalties, or royalties from the sale of recordings, to songwriters and publishers. This is generally done through the Harry Fox Agency, which collects monies from recording companies and pays them directly to the publishers who, in turn, pay the writers.

There is a statutory rate (in 1994 it was 6.6 cents per song or 1.25 cents per minute for songs over 5:15 minutes) but recording companies regularly request a 25 percent reduction in mechanical royalties if the artist writes his own material. These are called controlled compositions and most publishers grant this request, reasoning that the recording company will have more money to spend on promoting the artist and thus the copyrights so that income from publishing and songwriting will benefit in the long run. Also, the labels argue that they receive no money from radio and TV airplay.

Royalty Base Rate

The artist royalty rate may be based on retail or wholesale prices—this will vary from label to label and from contract to contract. Some artist contracts will have a "breakage allowance," a throwback from the days when a number of records broke in transit. This breakage allowance is generally 10 percent of the total number of units shipped. The royalty base rate is determined from computing the total number of albums sold minus the allowances, which—if the 10 percent breakage allowance and 10 percent packaging allowance is factored—would mean that the royalty base is 80 percent of the total number of units sold.

In order to reach the break-even figure in unit sales for an artist, the royalty amount per unit is divided into the total amount of recoupables. For example, if an artist makes $.50 in royalty for each album sold and if the label has invested $200,000 in recoupables, the artist must sell 400,000 albums before receiving royalties from album sales.

Producer's Royalties

In addition to royalties paid to an artist, most producers also receive royalties. The fee paid to the producer is usually a recoupable held against the artist's account. Thus the producer will not receive any royalties until the artist does. However, in some production deals, the producer will receive royalties from the first unit sold. Some in-demand producers charge a fee plus royalties from the first unit sold; others do not charge a fee but have royalties computed from the first unit sold. In the former case, the fee paid to the producer is a recoupable held against the artist in his/her account. However, most producers will not forego a fee as there is no guarantee any albums will be sold.

Other Recoupables or Charge-backs

Money spent on videos, independent promotion, advertising (TV and radio time buys and print placement), the manufacture of point-of-purchase (POP) materials such as posters, stand-ups and other items for retail displays, special contests, special promotions like talk tours where an artist visits cities to meet key retailers, radio personnel and others vital to marketing the product, money given for tour support and money given as an "advance" to cover living expenses may be charged back to the artist's account. This depends on the artist's contract—and will vary from contract to contract—but generally the artist will be charged for all expenses related to the production and marketing of his music.

Although the point where the artist has earned, through the accumulation of royalties based on the sales of their recordings, enough to pay back the label for charges the label has charged against their account is considered the break-even point, in fact the label's break-even point comes at a lower sales figure. To figure the break-even cost for the label, all money spent by the label should be added up—manufacturing, production, mechanicals for publishers (but not royalties to the artist, which are credited to the artist's account but not paid until the amount exceeds the recoupable costs) and then divided by the wholesale cost. For example, if a label spent $600,000 in order to release an album in the marketplace and it receives $8.50 wholesale for this album, it would take about 70,590 albums sold for the label to reach a break-even point. But if, on this same album, the artist had $300,000 in recoupables charged against their account and if the artist received $1.36 per album (based on a royalty rate of 16 percent of wholesale), the break-even point would be 220,588 albums sold. This means that, although the latter figure is used as the break-even point for a label and artist, in truth the label begins making a profit long before this. Thus artists who are considered money losers for a label may, in actual fact, be profitable for a label.

These rough computations about a label's break-even point do not take into account all their operating overhead (rent, mortgage, utilities, phone, salaries, warehousing, shipping) as well as normal promotion such as publicity press kits and promotion and possibly a few ads. For this reason the label continues to consider the artist's break-even point the actual break-even point for an album. That is why most labels say that it takes a Gold Record (sales on 500,000 units) before it can turn a profit on an album in the marketplace.

And that is why, from a strictly business perspective, a first album released by a new act is a bad investment; the odds are overwhelmingly against a new act showing a profit on a debut album. But there are business advantages even when an act loses money for the label. The 80 percent of the label's releases that may be considered break-even releases or even "flops" are important to a label because it tests the marketplace, lets the executives fine-tune their marketing skills and strategies, gives the company access to capital and credit, and gets it prepared to move into effective action when a smash album *does* come down the pike.

The recording industry is the only industry that charges its artists the entire cost of producing their work. This puts the ball in the label's court and allows them to function in this market with such high risk and high overheads and still remain a viable business. Since the recording company functions as a venture capitalist, they are inclined to invest in a number of acts in expectation on the big return from a few of these acts. These few acts make the whole venture profitable and worthwhile.

Also, it must be remembered when discussing album releases that only current releases have been mentioned. Although most of the time, effort, and energy at a recording company consists of dealing with current releases, the catalog of previously released albums for a company is very important. Some albums continue to sell years after their initial releases, some albums may be repackaged years later for income, and demands for an artist's catalog will soar if the act has a smash hit. Thus the label may be able to recoup part or all the costs of albums that have previously lost money. And the sheer volume of a catalog after the company has been in business for years and artists have released a number of albums generates a cash flow and constitutes a major asset that makes it valuable for the label and helps it overcome any losses from current releases.

Artwork

When a label schedules an album for commercial release, a certain amount of time is allotted for the musical production and a certain amount of time for the manufacturing. During this period, an album cover must also be developed.

Developing an album cover involves more than hiring a photographer to shoot some pictures, then picking the one that "turned out best" and putting it on the cover. The album cover will play an important part in the marketing of the album and the artist, so careful care and concern will be given to the image presented. This image should help define the artist and the label; sometimes a theme will be emphasized while other times there will be an emphasis on graphics or just a basic head shot of the artist. The photo session that yields the album cover may also be used as a source of photos for future advertising, including posters and other point-of-purchase material, and for publicity.

An image for the artist should be an extension of the person. It cannot be totally fabricated and last. When dealing with album artwork for a young artist, the key is to determine what this image is and work in that direction. When working to form this image, key elements should be emphasized while other elements are played down. This does not mean creating a whole new persona, but rather defining and fine-tuning what is already there, stressing strong points and covering up weaker points.

Consultation with a photographer and graphic artist should determine whether a photograph is the best way to present the artist, and if so, what the photograph should include. The graphic artist will also be concerned with layout and lettering. The back of the album is important, too, and a decision must be reached about what that should include. Since most compact discs contain a booklet, these contents should be discussed along with the layout to present it. If there is a title song that needs to be emphasized, or a theme running throughout the album, or a hit single to be emphasized, the artwork should take this into consideration.

Some artists feel their image should be developed inside the album with lyrics to songs, additional liner notes, additional pictures and perhaps even credits for songs, musicians, and additional personnel. For the artist whose looks are emphasized, there may be an abundance of pictures; for the artist who has something particular to say, there may be additional information to be presented. The problem with this internal packaging is that consumers are not able to see it while browsing in the store; for this reason, the cover of the album takes on added importance.

The photo session that produces the album cover should provide some alternatives for the label and artist so they can have a choice. A consensus must be reached between the artist, the label, and the photographer about the best photograph to present on the album cover; often four or five "dummy" album covers are marked up and examined before a final decision is made.

Some of these extra photographs—pictures made during the same session but slightly different from the album cover—may be used for point-of-purchase material or print advertising. The publicity department may use some of these photos since they need 8 x 10 black-and-white glossies for their press kits. Magazines often need a color transparency for a cover as well as other photos on the inside to illustrate a story on the act; often the publicity department will provide these photos.

In addition to the photos, there is also the question of graphics and colors, involving background as well as clothing. Obviously, the colors should flatter the artist and be compatible with whatever ideas or themes are being presented. All of this brings together several key concerns from the marketing department: *How will consumers notice this album in a store full of others and how well does this cover represent the image of the artist?*

Scheduling

The recording label would like for each album to be on the market at least a year in order to release several singles from the album and to maximize sales. This philosophy emerged in the 1980s and differs radically from the preceding idea of marketing whereby the label insisted the artist release two or three albums a year and that each album contain one (or at most two) hit singles. In the newer strategy of keeping an album on the market at least a year, the label treats the album as a brand new album each time a new single hits. This is because a consumer may not be moved to purchase the album from the first single, or even the second single. Perhaps it is the third or fourth single that convinces the consumer to purchase the album, either because the consumer likes that particular single enough to make a purchase or because the consumer feels he or she is getting a good deal with the collection of hit singles.

Timing is crucial to the success of a single and album. The most popular times to release albums are May and October; May is good for summer buyers, while October is targeted to those buying during the Christmas season. However, an obvious fact emerges: Every act cannot wait to release product during these times. Also, it is possible that a new, young act's debut album may be lost if their release is scheduled during this time.

The marketing department works with other departments of the label to determine the best time to release a single from an act. Factors that are considered include the other acts on the label, what other releases are scheduled, other acts at other labels who are releasing singles, and the constraints of the staff and their workload.

A single is expected to have an average life of 14 to 16 weeks if it is a hit; perhaps a few more weeks if it is a major hit, much less if it does not hit at all. Ideally, a new single on an act is released after the previous single has peaked and is beginning its descent on the charts. The act might have two singles on the charts at this time, one going up and the other coming off. If all goes according to plan, an act can comfortably release four singles during a single year and see them all achieve a successful life cycle of approximately 15 weeks.

There are problems with keeping an album on the market as a "new" album for a year or more. If the first or second single does not hit, then the marketing department of the label must determine whether it is wise to release more singles from the album. It is also possible that the singles can do well but the album not achieve major sales; at this point the company must reevaluate its own marketing strategies as well as the artist's image and activities to support the album.

An artist participates in a major campaign to market their album by scheduling a tour, making themselves available for press interviews, doing a video, and preparing special merchandise for the tour and the new album's release. A great many activities must be coordinated when an album is released to insure maximum exposure in the marketplace and to maximize consumer awareness of the act and their new product. This coordination is usually done by the act's manager, with important input from the recording label, booking agent, the artist, and others directly involved in the career of the artist.

Every act wants product constantly in the marketplace. If a single does not do well, the act would like another single shipped immediately; if an album does not sell well, they often want to record and release another album as soon as possible. This creates a constant dilemma for a recording label, which has a number of other artists on their roster. The staff at the label must try to balance a number of projects—singles and albums from a variety of acts—and try to insure they have given their best effort to each one. Scheduling the release of singles and albums from the roster's acts is a difficult job for label personnel because they must keep a constant level of excitement in each artist's career, must balance the demands of a number of artists, avoid lulls where no new product on an artist is available in the marketplace, and keep the careers of a number of acts moving forward.

The Marketing Plan

The marketing plan involves setting goals, strategies, and tactics for an act in the marketplace. Some goals may include reaching a certain sales plateau, obtaining a certain position on the trade charts (for singles and albums), performing in certain markets, and receiving exposure in specific media. All of these goals point toward achieving a measurable level of visibility in the marketplace.

Since the marketing department oversees and coordinates the activities of a number of other departments—promotion, publicity, advertising, sales—it will coordinate the activities of these departments when a marketing plan is implemented. Each of these departments may come up with its own goals for an act; in fact, each will be encouraged to develop goals. But it is the marketing department that oversees the execution of this plan in order to penetrate the marketplace and, ultimately, sell recordings to consumers.

The strategy of the marketing plan involves *how* the goals will be obtained while the tactics are the actual implementation of this plan, putting it into action with daily activities. It is important to have a plan for an act; without a plan, the act is at the mercy of daily events that can disrupt their career.

Budgets

Great ideas do not have to cost a lot of money; on the other hand, a lot of money invested in a marketing plan will not work if it is not a good idea to begin with. In drawing up a budget for a marketing plan the marketing department tries to spend as much money as it takes to implement an effective plan, but spend no money unnecessarily.

The first consideration in developing a budget for a marketing plan is the amount of money spent on studio production for the album. A label will usually allocate a certain amount of money for production and reserve a separate amount for marketing. However, if the production goes significantly over budget, the company must make a critical decision: should the marketing budget be cut back in order not to go over budget for the entire project, or should the budget be increased to reflect a better product and recoup the added investment.

Both choices have merit. For example, cutting back the marketing budget insures the label it will not lose a great deal of money if the product does not succeed in the marketplace. While artists and producers often feel angry and betrayed by such a decision—reasoning the extra production costs were necessary to make a top-notch recording—the company must look at the product more coldly. The passion of the artists and producers is understandable and even desirable. However, the label may reason that if the act is a new act with no track record and no hit single currently in the market, the odds are that increasing the budget is a bad risk financially. If, on the other hand, there is a hit single in the market the label may reason the product has been "tested" and consumers have accepted it, thus justifying an increased budget.

An act that is a proven seller with a record of past successes may be a good candidate for an increased budget. Also, if there is current success from this project—a hit single in the marketplace—the label may feel additional monies are well justified. But the point is that the company must have some reason to invest more money. Producers and artists are likely to insist the company should invest more money in marketing because more money was spent on production, or that, in an aesthetic sense the product is "better" because of the increased production costs, or because they believe in it fervently, based on their own passion, emotion, and involvement in the project, regardless of what initial market reaction might be. The marketing department must weigh all these factors in order to make an effective, intelligent decision to spend or not spend more money on an act.

On the other hand, an act whose studio production costs have come in significantly *under* budget also creates some interesting problems. On the psychological level, some marketing executives may feel the product cannot compete in the marketplace unless a certain amount of money is spent on production; the lesser amount of money indicates something is "wrong" with the album. Other marketing executives will perhaps rejoice at the low cost because this frees up more money for marketing the album. Artists may be perceived as shrewd and resourceful, aware of their own profit line, and more aware of the label's efforts on their behalf.

Artists sometimes attempt to manipulate the label into providing more marketing money by going well over budget in production costs. Their reasoning is that because the company has already spent so much money on the project, they will be reluctant to let it die and will work even harder—and spend more money—to insure it is a success. There is also the idea that the more money spent on something, the higher quality it is and therefore worth more effort and money for marketing. There is some merit to these arguments; a label is often reluctant to let a project "die" when there is so much invested in it. They would rather see success from sales to justify their investment; however, the label may also feel it is throwing good money after bad if there is no positive response from the market to justify additional expenditure. In other words, the company may feel pressured to minimize their losses rather than gamble on maximizing a potential success. If this is the case, the company will probably spend little if any money on marketing efforts until the product has managed to find its own way in the market and provide the label with some justification for more money.

Artists whose recordings have not been commercially successful often blame the company because not enough money was spent to insure success; on the other hand, artists whose product has been successful often credit the music itself for the success. Whenever artists discuss albums and singles that fail, there is usually the conclusion that it is the company's fault, generally because not enough money was spent on the product. But artists whose product has succeeded often concede that the marketplace has picked the winner, that consumers found their product appealing for some reason.

For record labels, staffed by people who love and care about music and artists, these are tough calls. But experienced label executives have all learned one important lesson: *you cannot buy a hit*. It does not matter how much money is poured into a project, if consumers don't like it—either at radio or retail—it will not be a hit. And if a recording has a genuine appeal at the consumer level, then it will succeed in the marketplace whether large sums of money have been spent or not. This is where the marketing departments must make their most critical decision: what product should have more money spent on it and which product should have the plug pulled?

Although each act is different and each project is different, certain grounds rules seem to emerge. First, if it is a new act with no past record of success there will probably not be an extensive marketing plan prepared for them by the company before the release of the project. For an act like this, the label will often adopt a "wait and see" attitude, trying to determine if the market accepts this act and his or her album or not. If there is reason to believe the act has been accepted, then the company can justify spending more money to boost the act toward the next level of success. If the act is a major act with an immediate past success, there will probably be an extensive marketing plan in place at the time of the album's release. This plan may be altered, amended, or adjusted as the new album and additional singles receive acceptance or rejection by the marketplace, but the company will generally commit to some amount of marketing money before the release.

For the act that has had some exposure in the market previously, but no great success, the label will probably develop a limited marketing plan, contingent upon some benchmarks being reached regarding exposure and media awareness. The company will want to let consumers know about the album but will not want to develop an extensive marketing plan until they see some acceptance from the marketplace. This is usually indicated by a hit single.

Price

The price for prerecorded product is set by the marketplace and by the recording labels. Generally, there is a "perceived value" of $10 to $15 for prerecorded product. Knowing this, the record companies generally stay within these parameters. The price of individual albums is *not* based on the cost of the album, but rather on prices of all other albums in the marketplace. For example, the label does not figure the cost of production, manufacturing, and all other costs for a particular album, project a sales figure, and divide the cost by the sales figure to determine price. Thus an album that costs $5,000 to produce and market will retail at the same general price as an album that cost $500,000 to produce and market. There are variations on prices for recorded product, especially with catalog items or repackaged product (especially boxed sets). For albums that have simply been repackaged—a new cover on the album or perhaps released in a new format—the costs of production have already been paid, so the label has only to pay manufacturing costs and mechanical income for publishers and songwriters, insuring a lower financial barrier to achieve a profit. There are also mid-line or discounted prices for albums, which have usually been re-released or have been in the market long enough to recoup initial costs. Re-releasing an album keeps it active and may stimulate additional sales.

Distribution

The distribution system for recordings carries music from the creators to the manufacturers to the outlet where consumers may buy them. The major labels all have their own in-house distribution system. This is known as label, in-house, or *branch* distribution. Although this distribution network is under the corporate umbrella, it is sometimes set up as a separate, distinct company whose sole role is to distribute product into the marketplace. The record company is thus free to find, develop, promote, and market talent while the distribution arm is in charge of penetrating the marketplace.

In the distribution system for major labels, the United States is divided into regions (generally five to eight) and then divided further into local markets, which includes roughly the top 20 markets nationally. The label will have a branch office in each of these cities.

Distribution begins at the manufacturing plant, where the two-track tape of an album has been produced as a retail product. The manufacturer ships the product into its system, where it is directed toward *rack jobbers* or *one-stops* who get the recordings into retail outlets. The rack jobber services "racks" or mass merchandisers, such as Kmart, Wal-Mart, Target, or any other high volume stores with a record section. These stores offer the top-selling 10 or 15 albums in the pop, country, and R & B music fields with limited catalog; they depend on high turnover for volume business. They can sell product for less because of the volume and because of the discounts they receive from doing volume purchases.

The one-stop services record stores. These companies take orders from individual record stores and supply the retailers with product from all the labels. It is a convenient way for a record outlet to get whatever recording it wants with one phone call. The major labels will personally service major accounts but do not want to deal with each individual store; because of the large number of record stores in this country, this would be a nearly impossible task.

The retailing industry for recordings is increasingly dominated by chain outlets, and these chain outlets often serve as their own one-stop—a central office will place orders from all the record companies and then supply each of their individual stores from this central location.

However, if a store cannot get a record from their central location, they will probably call a local one-stop. Even mass merchandisers like Wal-Mart have their own in-house distributor to serve their racks (It may be noted that one-stops *primarily* sell to record stores and rack jobbers *primarily* sell to racks—but not exclusively. Each can also sell to drugstores, convenience markets, or wherever else recordings are sold.)

It is from major labels, through their branch distribution system, utilizing one-stops and rack jobbers, that most recordings get to retailers; however, there is an alternative system. Independent distribution companies are in business to distribute recordings to wherever consumers buy recordings. This is where most small labels start and how much specialty music is distributed. These companies handle a variety of labels and many different types of music and work much the same way as a major label except they are confined to a particular city or region. Thus, an artist on a major label will be distributed to stores via an in-house network while an artist with a small independent label may be distributed by a number of independent distributors in order to be in retail outlets. Both in-house and independent distribution will use rack jobbers and one-stops, but the marketing director for an independently distributed company will have to deal with a number of different organizations to get their recordings in stores while the marketing director at a major label will deal only within that organization.

Most recordings are bought from mass merchandisers or record stores, but these are not the only sources for records. Record clubs account for about 10-15 percent of record sales. These recordings go from the distributor directly to the club, then are sent directly to the customer.

Television marketing is another outlet, generally for greatest hits and compilation albums. These recordings are usually leased from the label by an independently owned company, which packages them and arranges time buys on TV stations. Again, these recordings will go directly from the manufacturer to the packager to the consumer.

"Cutouts" are recordings that are no longer being manufactured, usually due to lack of retail sales. These recordings are returned to the manufacturer or label, which packages and sells them in bulk for a low per unit cost. The buyers do not know what they are getting—so it is very high risk and there are certain to be albums *nobody* wants. However, these recordings are sold in special displays for a relatively low but still competitive price so it is high profit for those that do sell. Cutouts should not be confused with "returns," which are recordings returned to the label because they are defective.

5

Retailers and Record Companies

There are basically two kinds of retail outlets for recordings: racks and record stores.

The racks, located in mass merchandisers, will generally stock only the top-selling 10 or 15 albums from country, rock/pop, and R & B. They usually buy directly off the trade charts and stock very little catalog. The catalog they do stock tends to be from top acts or recent bestsellers. They may have some cutouts but do not have an extensive series of multipriced product.

The racks appeal to continuous and noncontinuous buyers—those who will buy several albums a year on impulse, who want what they are hearing regularly on the radio, and who do not generally go out shopping just for an album. These people are generally in the 25 to 50 age group, which goes to mass merchandisers to buy a variety of things they need in their home and life. While there, they may see an album they want and purchase it.

Prices are generally lower at the mass merchandisers than anywhere else because they operate on quantity. There is a significant amount of country music sales here—most country albums are sold in mass merchandisers—but generally not as large a selection as is available in most record stores.

There are four types of record stores: (1) mall stores, (2) free-standing stores, (3) independent stores, and (4) megastores.

The record stores located in shopping malls are similar to racks (mass merchandisers) in that they have a small, limited amount of space, must appeal to a wide range of customers, and must have a high turnover of product because their rent is usually paid from a percentage of sales. Thus a store must have a large turnover of product to generate enough income for its lease to be renewed. The mall stores must appeal to the young buyer, age 10 to 19, as well as the drop-in buyer. There will be an emphasis on hit albums, more catalog than the racks, but not as extensive as other kinds of stores because of the limited space. Mall stores are often part of a chain.

Buyers in the 10-to-19 group often see the mall record store as a social center, particularly on Friday and Saturday nights, when they congregate with their friends. Too, many parents bring their teenagers to the mall with them, then shop elsewhere in the mall while the teenagers hang out at the record store. But the young buyer is not the only buyer in a mall store. The 25-to-50 age group will often be in the mall shopping, walk by the record store and drop in to see new selections or check to see if a desired album is available. The 50-to-65 age group will stop in mall stores not only to shop for themselves but also to buy a gift for their children or grandchildren. So the mall store must appeal to a wide variety of people who want different things.

The free-standing store appeals to the more dedicated record buyer. These stores either stand alone or in a small strip mall. The people who shop at these stores generally drive to the store just to look at and buy recordings. Unlike the mall store, there are not a lot of customers shopping at other stores for other consumer goods who drop in just to briefly check out the place.

The free-standing store will generally have a much better, more extensive catalog than the mall store. This store appeals to a more involved, committed buyer and thus the sales personnel are generally more knowledgeable and committed to the music. Many of these free-standing stores are also chain-owned.

The independent store may also be called a mom and pop. It is a store not owned by a chain and represents the entrepreneurial spirit of American business. Often these independent stores specialize in a particular type of music and reflect the personality of their owners. For example, an independent store may stock an extensive selection of classical product, or blues, or bluegrass depending upon the taste of the owner. In fact, many of these stores exist because the owner loves a particular kind of music and wants to make it available to consumers. For that reason, there will most likely be extensive catalog of the owner's choice of music. These stores may also serve as a clearing house for information about a particular music, supplying information on new product, concerts by acts, and as a center for people with similar tastes in music networking. Musicians often frequent these stores to meet other musicians.

The megastore reflects the trend in American retailing whereby shopping at one place allows consumers to find a large and deep selection of merchandise. These stores offer an extensive catalog on all kinds of music, often dividing the store into rooms or sections where different kinds of music are available. These appeal to consumers who love music and want to be surrounded by it as well as to consumers who want only to find a non-current album that cannot be found elsewhere The store is particularly appealing to fans of specialty musics like folk, blues, bluegrass, jazz, and classical, which do not sell enough product to be stocked in mass merchandisers or mall stores. Buyers of these musics are able to find otherwise difficult-to-find albums, older product, and extensive catalog on particular artists or musics. This store will have more inventory than any other kind of record store and will stock more kinds of music. Its success is dependent upon supplying product that music-buying consumers cannot find anywhere else.

Another kind of record store has emerged in the mid-1990s. The "theme store" (also known as the "big box" or "category buster") has a large inventory connected to "entertainment," which includes recordings, videos, and books. These stores are "one-stop-shopping" for those interested in entertainment. As the malls have declined in the 1990s and the stand-alone stores have proliferated, the success stories in retailing belong to these stores (like Home Depot, Toys R Us, and MediaPlay). These stores have large inventories and don't just sell a "product" but the adventure for shopping for a product as well. Trends suggest that these "theme stores" will become more dominant in retailing as the mall stores decline in importance.

Appeal

What makes a record store appealing to consumers? There are a number of factors, but the first appeal is location. Simply put, people tend to shop at the place that is most convenient. For some that means a mall store; for others that means a free-standing store close to their home.

Another appeal is price. Virtually no retailer of current recorded product sells for "suggested retail price" because they must remain competitive and attract consumers who are likely to be able to go to a variety of record stores. But as long as price is competitive, this will not be the major factor governing consumers' behavior. Generally, the racks sell for less than any other stores, while the independents and megastores charge more.

Service is important, especially for the independents and megastores, which depend upon knowledgeable sales personnel to help consumers. For the mall stores, service usually involves allowing consumers to browse. Special promotions such as contests and artist visits and signings will attract consumers to a store. Some stores, in fact, seek to create a reputation of being a place where something is "always happening."

Advertising in the media is another way record stores attract consumers, letting them know what product is available or if there is a special sale or promotion. Advertising helps a store develop a particular image which hopefully makes it distinct from other record retailers. In-store airplay can provide a conducive atmosphere for consumers to browse and shop as well as stimulating sales for the recording being played. People want to hear their favorite music in the store. This makes it difficult for mall stores because they have such a wide variety of consumers. However, the independents often expose their customers to new product or favorite acts through in-store airplay and free-standing stores may do the same.

In-store layout, design, and decorations such as posters, mobiles, and stand-ups also serve as an appeal to consumers. The way a store looks, how it is laid out, and the information a consumer receives from material on the wall or on display—all help create an atmosphere and image to appeal to the patrons of a particular record store.

The Retailer's Perspective

The marketing department at a recording label must answer the central question of how and why stores stock particular records and ignore others. The sales force at the label obviously must make product available in stores in order for sales to occur. On the other hand, few stores are able to stock everything released and thus choices must be made by retail managers about which product to stock and which not to stock. Several factors go into this decision:

1. *Hit record.* If the recording is a hit, the retailer must stock it. If it is being played in heavy rotation on the radio, the store generally cannot ignore it.

2. *Major artist.* For a major artist with a good track record for sales, new product from that artist will be stocked because fans will want to buy the new recording as soon as it is released.

3. *Major label release.* The mall stores and free-standing stores are likely to stock an album if it is released by a major label, particularly if it is in the major categories of rock/pop, country and R & B. Because the major labels have such a pervasive and effective distribution system, with personal relationships developed with key wholesalers and retailers, they are usually able to get their product stocked.

4. *Customer request.* This involves a manager's knowing the store's clientele, what kind of music they like, and what they are looking for. If a number of customers request an album or artist not generally stocked, the manager will probably begin stocking them.

5. *Artist publicity tour.* If an artist is scheduled to make a major appearance—or perhaps has made one—in the area, the store is likely to stock their product because an appearance often generates interest and demand for product.

6. *Other kinds of artist exposure.* These include appearances on major concerts that receive wide coverage, soundtracks to popular movies, appearances on television, or perhaps major coverage in print. All of these generate interest in an artist that can generate sales if product is available.

7. *Exposure on local radio.* College radio stations, especially, may play more esoteric artists or music not on the charts, and a following for an artist may be developed from this airplay. It is also possible that a local radio station may be playing product not on the charts but which is creating a local "buzz" and following for a song or artist.

8. *Store manager's interest.* Particularly with independent stores, a store manager will stock an artist he or she is

interested in. However, it is also possible in free-standing stores that the particular taste of a store manager will have a bearing on some of the product stocked and some other product being ignored.

9. *Influence of record company.* If a record company sales person has an ongoing relationship with a store manager, the manager may be influenced to stock albums from that company that are not hits or artists who are not major artists. This relationship evolves from contact between the store manager and record company representative and is nurtured by the record company representative's supplying information about new releases as well as perquisites such as concert tickets, promotional copies of albums, and other special promotions developed by the label.

The Record Company

The record company must establish relationships with record retailers so that when new product is made available, the store will be induced to stock it before a sales track record has been established. There are a number of ways a label establishes and continues a successful relationship with record retailers:

1. *Contact with the store.* This is the major way record companies insure good relations with retail outlets—by constant and consistent contact with store managers, finding out what their needs are, informing them what new product is available, and establishing a relationship of trust.

2. *Co-op advertising.* This involves record companies and stores splitting the costs of advertising. This may occur in several ways. Often the label will give an amount of money to a rack jobber to make available for ads. For chains, the label may give a cash inducement to the head office to be distributed to the local stores as it sees fit. Or a label may deal directly with a record store, supplying mock ads, helping with the placement of these ads, and paying a

portion of the costs. In almost all cases, the label does not direct these advertisements to specific media; the retailer generally has control of when and where these advertisements run.

3. *Promotional copies of albums.* The label often supplies promotional copies of new albums to stores to use for in-store airplay. If an album is not supplied, the store must use a copy of one they have purchased for in-store airplay, thus losing the possibility of selling that album to a consumer. For a new act, where perhaps only one or two copies of an album are stocked, in-store airplay will probably not be generated unless free promotional copies are made available.

4. *Promotional videos.* Again, stores often show videos in their stores. Labels will often supply these videos to obtain exposure for their acts.

5. *In-store contests.* If a label is sponsoring a particularly appealing in-store contest—involving good prizes or if there is a good likelihood of a store winning something—then the retailer is more likely to become involved with the product and stock it as well as put up an attractive display.

6. *In-store materials.* These include posters, mobiles, stand-ups, and other material to use for displays. These may or may not be linked to an in-store contest. Particularly appealing are bin cards, which list the artist's name on a large bin divider which a store may use to separate that artist's recordings from others and make it easy for consumers to find them.

7. *Providing artists.* This may involve making sure an artist stops by a store during a concert appearance in an area or for a special promotion that the store is running. Usually the artist signs copies of their albums for consumers who visit the store.

8. *Special promotions.* Some labels have run campaigns in which they give a store an instant prize (such as cash) if a

label representative stops by the store and one of the label's recordings is being played over the store system. Or perhaps a store may receive T-shirts, caps, and buttons for a special push on an act or other trinkets and incentives in order to catch the attention of a store manager.

6

Radio and Record Labels

The major function of promotion at a recording label is getting records played on the radio. To do this, the promotion person spends most of his or her time on the telephone, calling radio stations and giving them information to convince the program and music directors to play the records being promoted. Basically, there are six steps to promoting a record.

1. *Supply the product.* This means making sure the radio stations receive the recordings. It also means sending them to the trade magazines and other key media for reviews.

2. *Follow up.* After the records have been received, the promotion person wants to get a reaction from the program and music directors. This lets the programmers know that someone is interested in the recording and encourages them to listen and make a decision about the product.

3. *Supply information.* The information a promotion person supplies about a recording includes how it is doing on the national charts, the sales activity, how it is doing in other markets, whether there is a major promotional push from the label, whether the act is touring in the area, and anything else that helps the programmer make a decision about whether to program this record on the station.

4. *Serve as liaison* between the radio station, record label, and artist. The promotion person, by communicating with all three of these parties, is in a strategic position to let each know what the other's reactions are to new product. The promotion person is in the unique position of serving as a

conduit between the label and radio about trends in the marketplace; he or she can also communicate with the artist to arrange interviews or special promotions.

5. *Check sales.* Although all the singles charts do not factor in sales for chart positions, a record must generate sales in order to be successful. Too, sales are a good indicator of the acceptance of a record. Therefore, the promotion person will make sure recordings are available in a market that is playing a record, will inform programmers of significant sales of a particular record, and will make sure that a record being played will generate income for the label by ensuring it is available to consumers.

6. *Work surrounding stations.* If a major reporting station is reluctant to program a record, a major way to convince them to play the record is for other stations in the listening area to play it. Too, the goal of a promotion person is to have the recording played on every single radio station, so he or she will try to make sure that stations other than just the reporting stations are playing the record.

The Promotion Network

There are two basic kinds of promotion in the music industry: label (staff or in-house) and independent promotion.

The staff promotion person works for the record company as a paid employee. The structure at a major label usually has promotion divided into national, regional, and local. There is usually a national promotion person for rock, country, and R & B music. These people are in charge of all product released by the label in their respective area of music. Under them are regional promotion people, usually five to eight, who are in charge of a particular kind of music (rock, country, R & B) in an area of the country.

There are also approximately 20 to 30 local promotion persons at each major label. Each local promotion person is responsible for *all* the product released by the label in their specific market. This means that while the national and regional people will only be involved with R & B music, or rock, or country, the local person will have every kind of music the label releases—rock, classical, jazz, country, R & B, easy listening, et al.—and be responsible for getting all of them exposure on the radio. Therefore the job of the national and regional promotion people at the label often involves lobbying the local person to impress upon them the importance of promoting specific product.

All radio stations are not created equal. The "reporting stations" are more important than all the other stations because these are the stations which report their playlists to the national trades, who compile the national charts from these playlists. Therefore, the playlist at a reporting station has more significance than those of a non-reporting station because it directly affects the ranking of recordings on the national charts. For that reason, a major job for the national promotion person is to keep in close contact with all reporting stations and try to influence them to play and report their product.

The regional promotion person is also in contact with a number of reporting stations, although limited to their own region, while the local promotion person, obviously aware of the reporters—and involved heavily with them—has the added task of making sure that every station in a market is playing a particular record.

Within each market, some stations that are not reporters are more important than others. The relative importance of radio stations is based on ratings in the market, strong signals, and hence a wider range. Such stations are particularly influential because of their success with a segment of the market or because they are willing to go on untested records and provide a testing ground for the national success of a recording.

The advantages to the staff promotion person in working a record include the following:

1. *Can supply "perks" (or perquisites).* This means the "goodies" that a record company gives away, such as free albums and other paraphernalia (such as T-shirts, caps, and promotional gimmicks and trinkets) as well as concert tickets, access to acts when they are in a market, and quicker service on releases.

2. *Has a regular paycheck, office, and telephone.* The company pays these expenses so they don't come out of an individual's pocket.

3. *Always has records to promote.* The label is constantly releasing recordings, so there is always product to call about.

4. *Can generally get closer to acts, producers, and others directly involved in the recording.* This helps when giving information to the radio stations and feedback to the creative side about the reactions to recordings.

5. *Job does not usually depend on how well the last record did.* The job does not totally depend upon the success of a single release; there is the benefit of working a number of releases.

The disadvantages are that a staff promotion person—

1. *May become too close* to *the creative people.* This perhaps puts them under the gun to deliver success for a recording that is *not* a hit.

2. *Has to deal with recordings and artists they do not necessarily like or believe in.* With so many acts and so many recordings, there will be some the promotion person is just not excited about but must still give time and effort to.

3. *Has to deal with problems of office politics and other office situations.* A lot of time will be spent meeting people, writing memos, and other activities that must be done within a company but are not directly related to getting records played on the radio. These activities can drain valuable time and energy.

4. *Often has too many records to promote.*

The advantages to the independent promotions person are that he or she—

1. *Is independent.* This means that all the advantages and motives from being in business for themselves and possessing the entrepreneurial spirit come into play.

2. *Is self-motivated.* This ties in with No. 1 and adds an energy and excitement to the job.

3. *Can work only those records they are excited about.* The top promotion people may choose which records they will work and which they will turn down. If they don't feel a record has the potential to be a hit, they will turn it down—and since their credibility rests heavily on delivering "winners," this can be a critical part of their job.

4. *Can spend more time with radio personnel.* Since the independent generally does not have the distractions that a label promotion person has, he or she is able to spend more time on the phone with radio stations working records and developing relationships with program directors.

5. *Can provide more objectivity.* Although independents are paid to promote recordings, the fact that they don't *have* to promote whatever records a company releases provides them an objectivity that label promotion people do not have.

The disadvantages are that an independent promotion person—

1. Has *limited resources,* particularly financial resources. Since all expenses for doing business must be paid by the proprietor, every phone call made, every letter sent, as well as office rent and supplies, must be paid for out of pocket.

2. *Generally cannot supply the "perks"* that a label promotion person can supply. Boxes of albums and other freebies from a label are generally unavailable to the independent promotion person, unless they pay for it themselves.

3. *Must sometimes struggle for records to promote.* As in any other business, there will be times when the independent is

extremely busy and other times when he or she has to find a way to pay the bills. This may involve time spent soliciting recordings to promote—and, if recordings are not available, the business will suffer.

4. *Lacks a label's name and connections.* Radio stations may be reluctant to accept the calls of an independent promotion person. Since stations will always have an ongoing relationship with major labels—and because they depend upon these labels so much for product service as well as other perquisites—the stations will always take the calls of the label promotion people and consider the records for "adds." However, since the independent promotion person has only his or her own integrity and reputation, some radio stations may be reluctant to talk to "indies."

From the label's standpoint, independent promotion people are vital because they give extra support in promotion, helping get the record on the radio station. However, they are much more difficult to control and the label sometimes does not know if the recording is actually being promoted, how it is being promoted, and whether the independent promotion efforts are effective.

Radio

The primary function of a radio station is to gain an audience. It does this through public services, contests, on-air personalities, news, special features—and the music it plays.

There is a synergistic relationship between the record industry and radio—they need each other. Radio needs the music produced by record labels to attract an audience, and the labels need radio because this exposure creates a demand for recordings that result in sales, which in turn provide the income for keeping the label in business. However, there is an adversarial relationship as well, and the labels and radio find themselves going in opposite directions while needing the other to get there.

Labels consistently complain that radio should program more new acts, take chances with more new releases, or program some older acts that the label feels are still viable but which radio, in their quest for a young audience, is often reluctant to program. Radio counters that labels should release more hits and be more cognizant of the radio audience—and more receptive to radio input—when determining which recordings to release. The basic problem is that there are two entirely different purposes at work here: radio wants to gain an audience, the record labels wants to sell recordings. Sometimes these purposes can blend and be mutually beneficial; at other times, these different purposes cause major problems and conflicts in the working relationship between radio and record companies.

This conflict often leads to a standoff: the problems of selling recordings are of no concern to the radio station while the problems of attracting an audience to a particular radio station are of no concern to the label. This results in a symbiotic relationship between labels and radio.

Ratings and Shares

Radio generally divides the day into "shifts," which correspond to the time slots used by broadcast measurement companies. From 6 to 10 a.m. is *morning drive;* from 10 a.m. to 3 p.m. is *mid-day;* from 3 p.m. to 7 p.m. is *afternoon drive;* from 7 p.m. to 12 midnight is *evening;* and from midnight to 6 a.m. is *late night* or *all night.*

Within these categories, ratings are broken down into quarter hours or 15-minute time periods. For a station, the average quarter hour shows what percentage of the population are listening during this time. *Cume,* or *cumulative, ratings* and *shares* tell what percentage of the population listens at least once during the time period; that is, the number of people listening over a long period of time (usually a week).

Share indicates which people were listening to a particular station out of those in an area listening to radio. Some other terms to know when discussing radio audiences: *average persons:* the number of people listening to a particular radio station; *metro average persons:* the number of people listening to radio (all stations) in a given market.

It is interesting to note that when the ratings for radio appear in a market, a number of stations claim to be "No. 1" in the market. In essence, this claim depends upon what market they are aiming for. For example, one radio station may attract the greatest number of 10-19-year-olds, while another has the greatest number of 35-50-year-olds. Or one station has the highest numbers from 7 to 7:15 in the morning while another attracts the largest audience throughout the day. Some radio stations aim for the people driving to work in the morning and afternoon, while other stations want to attract listeners (like those in offices) who turn their radio on in the morning and keep it on the same station all day long. This directly relates to advertising revenue: if a station can convince advertisers it is reaching the audience for a product at the time the advertiser wants them to be reached, then the business will purchase advertising time, creating revenue for a station.

Programming

It is a supposition of many people not in the music industry that a great recording will always rise to the top. These people believe that when a great recording arrives at a radio station, someone will listen to it, put it on the air, and the audience will respond. Unfortunately, this is an erroneous assumption.

First, most radio stations do not listen to *everything* they receive. There are several reasons for this. There just isn't enough time. If the recording is on a small label with no distribution by an artist with no track record, the likelihood is that it is not a hit if decisions are made based on percentages. Too, even if this is a great recording and is programmed, if the consumers cannot buy it they will feel frustrated and angry. But they will not be mad at the label or the artist or the distribution network—they will most likely be angry at the radio station for playing a recording that can't be purchased. So the station has a lot to lose even if these recordings are a hit.

Finally, the station will not listen simply because no one calls about the recording. They may be filled with good intentions, intending to listen to everything and perhaps giving a cursory listen to most product which comes in, but unless a promotion person (or someone else) calls and questions them about the recording, there is no real impetus for them to listen. This is why promotion is so vital to the success of a recording.

The accusation generally comes: the radio stations always listen to releases from the major labels. Yes, that's basically true for several reasons:

1. There is a proven track record of a major label for providing hits.

2. The distribution network is established so that if a station plays a recording they may be assured that retail stores either have copies or can obtain them easily.

3. The promotion departments of major labels have ongoing relationships with program directors, so when a recording arrives on a program director's desk, he or she is assured that soon there will be a phone call asking about the reaction to the record as well as for a decision about whether or not this recording is going to be programmed.

Having said that, it must be noted that every year there are a few recordings—perhaps an average of five annually—which are deemed "natural hits." These recordings, almost all on major labels, gain immediate acceptance at radio and then with consumers. These are the joys of the industry and every label is thankful when it has one of these; however, for the most part, the success or failure of recordings at radio depends upon the effectiveness of the label's promotion staff.

Radio Programming

In looking at the decision of whether or not to program a recording from the radio programmers' point of view, certain factors are weighed in their decision on whether or not to program the recording on their station:

1. *Is it on the national trade charts?* Since the United States is a nation of "national" trends and tastes, what is doing well in other parts of the country will tend to be appealing in a particular market. Also, this is a way to "measure" the success of a record; if it does well in another market, it is likely to do well in the home market.

2. *Names* (sometimes known as "hits and heroes"). The major acts develop strong followings who want to hear their next record. This creates a "built-in" demand for top name acts, although this demand will not last forever.

3. *The competition.* If a radio station's major competitor in a particular market is playing a certain record, then that station is more likely to play it too.

4. *Requests.* Radio stations may get requests for a recording even if they are not playing it because although listeners tend to have a favorite station, they listen to a number of other stations and may have heard the recording on another station. Since listeners generally do not know the playlists for individual stations, the assumption is that a hit record is being played on their favorite radio station and, when they call a station to make a request, it is their favorite station they call, even if that particular station is not playing the recording.

5. *Sales.* If a particular record or act is selling well in an area (this can be checked by calling local record stores), this

shows a demand from consumers for this record or act and a radio station will want to be aware of this and program to suit this demand.

6. *Call-out research.* Many top radio stations don't wait for listeners to call them; instead, these stations regularly engage in "call-out" research whereby they call people in the listening audience and ask about various recordings or reaction to special promotions or even the radio station in general. This call-out research can reveal especially negative or positive responses to artists and/or recordings.

7. *Program or music director's decision.* On occasion, a programmer will decide to program a record simply because he or she likes it. It is rare, but not impossible, for a programmer to venture out on a limb and do this, although most are reluctant to do so. The basic reason is that they may be wrong and program a record that is a "tune-out" factor. A tune-out factor is anything that causes a listener to change the station. It could be a commercial, a disc jockey, news, a traffic report—or a recording.

8. *Promotion person.* By being informative and persuasive, a promotion person may convince a programmer to put a particular record on the playlist of a radio station. This is the reason promotion people exist and the good ones are particularly adept at doing this.

(Note: Another way radio stations are programmed is through consultants, who rely heavily on research methods such as focus groups to recommend the playlists for a station. Some of these consultants offer a computer program to determine what recordings to play, how often they should be played, and the mix of up-tempo to ballad or oldies to current releases for a station. Although these consultants are powerful and pervasive, their methods of programming radio are not discussed at length here.)

Arbitron

Arbitron is a broadcast measurement company which specializes in measuring the success of radio stations. They are similar to the Nielsons for TV and their results are commonly called ARB's. These ARB's divide an audience into categories, generally called "demographics." Demographics is the study of populations and categorizes them in relation to age, sex, race, and other definable categories. (According to the *American Heritage Dictionary* [1992] and *Random House Unabridged Dictionary* [1993], demographics are "the characteristics of human populations" or "the statistical data of a population"; demography is the study of such data. This is comparable to "psychographics," which collects data on people's tastes, habits, and preferences.)

Two important terms to know when talking about broadcast measurement are ratings and shares. A rating is based on the total population of a listening area while a share is based on those listening to radio at a particular time. To determine the rating of a particular station, take the number of listeners for that particular station (Average Persons) and divide that by the total population of an area (AP divided by P = R). To measure the share for a station, divide average persons by the total number of people listening to radio at a particular time (Metro Average Persons). That formula is (AP divided by MAP = S). Ratings and shares are broken down into demographic categories so that each radio station knows the age, sex, race of their listeners during each time category (average quarter hours) or overall during an extended period of time (cume, short for cumulative).

Charts

The "charts" found in trade magazines are important to the recording industry because they provide a weekly barometer on how well singles and albums are doing in the national market. For those who work in promotion and sales, the charts are a quantification of how well they do their jobs. For booking agents and concert promoters, the charts indicate who is hot and who is not, and thus determine value in the marketplace for personal appearances. For publishers and songwriters, the charts indicate the acceptance of their copyrights in the marketplace and therefore they can project their potential earnings; for recording labels, the charts are the measuring stick whereby they measure their successes and failures relative to other labels in the marketplace.

Since charts are so important—and often misunderstood—it is appropriate to provide a working definition of charts. (Actually, there are two different definitions, one for singles and one for albums, but they will be combined into one statement.) The definition for a chart is: *A numerical ranking of current releases based on sales and airplay over a one week period of time.*

The *numerical ranking* simply means that the top rated song/album is No. 1 and the rest are listed in descending order, ranked correspondingly. *Current releases* means that only current product is tracked—not oldies. Therefore, even though an old recording may get more airplay during a particular week than the current No. 1, it will not be on the charts. *Current releases* are generally defined for the singles charts as 26 weeks after the release; in the event it is an old recording that has been re-released, the "current" definition applies from the time it is re-released. (This sometimes happens with movie soundtracks, when an old recording is on the soundtrack album and used as a single.)

Sales and airplay is where the difference noted earlier comes into play. The singles charts are based on airplay while the album charts are based on sales. These two categories, *single releases* and *album product,* are the two essentially different types of charts, although there are charts for a number of different kinds of music. The major difference between the two types of charts is whether single recordings, or individual songs, are tracked or whether albums are tracked. For the singles charts, reports come from reporting stations, or radio stations who report their airplay to the trades for the compilation of the national charts. For the album charts, reports come from wholesalers and retailers (also called reporters) whose information on sales is used to compile the national charts.

The *one week period* is the time between the calculation of one chart and the gathering of information for the compilation of the next one. Thus, if a recording does well over a long period of time (slow and steady sales) it will not do as well on the charts as will a recording which sells a lot of copies (or receives a lot of airplay) during a one week period of time.

The way the charts are compiled is called the *methodology* and the methodology differs between competing trade magazines. With *Billboard,* before 1990 the methodology for singles charts involved collecting playlists and reports from reporting stations and assigning numerical value for each position on the chart. After figuring how many points a recording received for being in that particular position on the reporting station's chart, *Billboard* then multiplied those points by the weight of the station. This weight was determined by the strength of the station in the market as well as the size and strength of the market itself.

After 1990, *Billboard* created a new data collection company, Broadcast Data System, to collect information about what is being played on radio stations. It collects this information through computer sampling, monitoring, and identifying each song played via an encoded audio "fingerprint." According to *Billboard,* the BDS computers can also provide data on demographics and market share such as quarter-hour shares of the stations and listener profiles. With this new methodology, the BDS system is installed in primarily large and medium market stations. It counts the number of times each record is played on each of these stations and then multiplies the play by the number of listeners using broadcast measurement data. These totals, called *gross impressions*, are then ranked numerically to determine the chart. *Bullets*, which are actually markings on the chart to indicate all titles showing a significant increase in gross impressions, are awarded to recordings that are rapidly gaining acceptance in the marketplace and thus moving up the chart. *Billboard*'s monitoring cycle runs from Monday to Sunday of each week; every Monday the information from radio stations is downloaded into a central data bank where the total number of points for each single is compiled and the relative rankings are determined. *Radio and Records* (*R&R*), a competing trade magazine, continues to rely on reports from radio station playlists, with each radio programmer telling *R&R* whether a song is in "heavy," "medium," or "light" rotation. Using a weighting method whereby stations in major markets and with larger audiences are given greater "weight," the *R&R* charts are then compiled. What differentiates the *R&R* charts from *Billboard*'s charts is the use of computer technology as well as *R&R*'s policy of asking radio stations their plans for the future airplay the following week. Thus, while *Billboard*'s charts tell exactly what was played the past week, *R&R* attempts to combine what was played the previous week as well as what is being played while readers are examining *R&R*'s charts.

Album charts are compiled from sales reports received from retailers, rack jobbers, and distributors. Before 1990, *Billboard* took these reports over the phone, with the reporters giving relative rankings based on success at their company. Again, a point amount was assigned according to the ranking of these sales reporter's charts and this point amount was multiplied by the weight of the sales reporter—usually based on volume of sales—for the total points. However, after the fall of 1990, *Billboard* began to use a company called SoundScan, which collects data from retail sales based on bar code scanners and then downloads this data into a central bank where actual sales figures are used to compile the relative rankings of album charts.

The use of computer technology to determine actual airplay and actual sales has had a profound impact on the recording industry. There are no longer any secrets with sales and airplay in the industry—anyone who subscribes to *Billboard*'s BDS network or SoundScan's data services can receive information about what is being played and what has been sold in the marketplace within the past week.

Prior to the use of computer technology, the charts were subject to manipulation because of the prejudices of reporters, inaccurate reporting, and the influence of promoters and marketers who could affect reporters and the information that was provided. The new methodology has been especially beneficial to country music, which had suffered from reporter bias during the non-computer reporting period. This was manifested by reporters *not* reporting country sales on the same charts as pop music sales and thus country sales were underreported. Since many buyers at the rack jobbers, wholesalers, and retailers buy directly from the charts, reasoning that success creates more success and thus what has proven itself in the market via sales will create greater sales with additional exposure, country music languished. Since it was not on the pop charts, it was considered a small market; when it did have major sales (and a number of acts did have big sales in country music), it was still relegated to the back of the store. But the switch to computer technology proved to those selling music that country music was a major seller, competing with major pop acts. And so they stocked more country, making it more visible, which in turn generated even greater sales. The image of country music as the hayseed stepcousin to the world of pop music was replaced with country music as the music of choice for a large number of consumers.

Problems with the Charts

Although charts have become more accurate because of the raw data gathered from radio airplay and retail sales, which indicate exactly what is being played or sold and not someone's interpretation of these sales and airplay, there are still problems with the charts. First, charts are inferential computations, which means that a small sample is taken in order to determine a large number—computations of airplay and sales from a relatively small number of reporters can imply what the nation as a whole is listening to and buying.

There is nothing inherently wrong with using a small sample in order to determine a large number; in fact, it is done in opinion sampling all the time. When pollsters announce that 54 percent of the population will vote for a certain candidate or agree with a certain issue, they have not asked the entire population of the United States; instead, they have asked a small, representative sample—usually only a few thousand—and computed their results from these. However, the major difference in the methodologies of the opinion samplers and chart compilers is that the opinion samplers use a *random data base* while those compiling the charts use a *fixed data base*.

This fixed or constant data base is the reporting stations, which are used each week by the trades for the compilation of their charts and known to the industry. Since the recording labels and independent promotion people know which radio stations are reporters, they concentrate their efforts toward influencing these stations. Obviously, this practice has the potential to skew the results because the reporting radio stations are treated differently than non-reporting stations; promotion people regularly develop close relationships with reporting stations but generally do not even call the non-reporters.

Another problem with the charts is that, because of the technology used, the reporting stations are those in major markets. Since approximately 80 percent of the American population lives in urban markets, this may not be a problem; however, the fact that 20 percent of the population live in rural areas and that these areas are not represented in the sample used for the charts indicates the potential for chart inaccuracy.

The problem of fixed vs. random data base is one the recording industry has chosen to accept. If the recording industry did chose to have a random data base, it would in essence dismantle an important aspect of the industry—radio promotion—and thousands would be out of a job. However, the performing rights organizations do random-based surveys to determine which songs are being performed most often. At the end of each accounting period they usually discover that some songs that did very well on the charts did not get as much airplay as others that did not have as much chart success; too, they find a number of oldies got a significant amount of airplay, sometimes more than a current hit. However, these oldies would never be on the charts because of the basic definition of the charts: a numerical ranking of *current releases* based on sales and airplay over a one-week period of time.

Another aspect of this definition of the charts—*a one-week period of time*—provides another way the charts may not be totally accurate. An example: suppose a current act releases an album that sells 10,000 copies a week for six straight weeks. An older, established act on the other hand releases an album that sells 2,000 copies a week but sells this amount for 52 weeks. The hot new act would have the best chart position—but at the end of the year the accounting department would like the older act better because it sold 104,000 vs. 60,000 for the new act. Thus the lack of consideration for long-term sales may be a detriment for a totally accurate chart.

A final reason the charts may be skewed is that sales reports are only taken from mainstream outlets; that is, record stores, mass merchandisers, one-stops and rack jobbers. If an album sells a million copies via TV sales, or from direct mail, or through merchandising at concerts, these sales are not reflected on the charts. Although the great majority of albums are sold through mainstream outlets, there is the problem of accurately determining the relative success of non-mainstream music sold through non-mainstream outlets. Examples here include a number of specialty musics.

7

Publicity and Advertising in the Media

It should be emphasized that there is a major difference between publicity and public relations and that, while publicity is a part of public relations, the latter includes much more than just publicity. To clarify this point, a definition of the role of publicists is provided. That role is to *provide information controlled by the source that is factual, interesting, and newsworthy to the media.* In practical terms, the *function* of publicists is to get their clients exposure in the media. In the recording industry, these clients are recording artists, although some music industry publicists also represent songwriters, label executives, and firms.

The flow of information from the client to the media is controlled by the publicist, who is either an employee of a client or an independent person or firm hired by the client in order to obtain media exposure for the client. This person is not objective but rather has the best interests and goals of the client in mind. This should not make him or her an adversary of the journalist, who seeks all sides of a story or issue, but someone who provides a service to the journalist. These services may include arranging interviews with a client, supplying information about a client, serving as a liaison between the client and the journalist, and making the journalist aware of the client and his or her newsworthy actions, activities, and events. Thus, the publicist is the liaison between the media and the client and gets the client exposure in the media by calling attention to, informing the media about, and persuading the media to cover the client.

Some of the duties of the publicist are writing press releases, photo captions, bios, putting together press kits, organizing press conferences, doing tour publicity, and preparing clients for interviews with the media. In day-to-day activity, providing tour publicity consumes most of the working publicist's time and efforts.

Strategy

In directing the efforts of publicity, there are two directions for publicists to focus their energies on when marketing an act; the first is publicity directed toward the industry and the second is publicity directed toward consumers.

When publicists direct information toward the recording industry, they target employees at the label, retail outlets, radio stations, trade magazines, bookers, concert promoters, journalists, and anyone else actively involved in the music industry who can help an act receive exposure to consumers. There are several key areas within the recording industry that need information about an act being publicized and marketed:

1. *Label personnel.* The people working at a label must be aware of their label's acts and recordings in order to be actively involved in marketing this act. These employees include everyone from field promotion and marketing people to other members of the publicity department and even people in accounting and business affairs. Since all of these people will eventually have a direct involvement in the act, this must be the very first step in marketing the act. Obviously, the recording label must be united in its efforts to promote and market an act, so in-house publicity generally means sending cassette copies of the single or album as well as a one page flyer about the act to employees.

2. *Radio.* Usually it is the promotion department who inform key radio personnel about new acts and new product. However, if bios and press kits are to be sent, or on-air interviews arranged, then the publicity department becomes involved.

3. *Retailers.* Promotional copies of an album as well as other print material such as bios, pictures, and reprints of news stories and reviews will be sent to retailers to make them aware of an act and/or recording so they will want to stock the recording as well as be informed when customers ask about the act or recording.

4. *Print media.* Since the print media will potentially write articles about a performer, giving consumers and other media their initial information about an act, they must be sent promotional copies of albums for reviews as well as press kits containing bios and pictures. This is particularly true for the trade press—*Billboard, Radio and Records* and *The Gavin Report*—because they cover the industry and the first exposure an artist receives is from the trade press through stories about signings, reviews, and label stories about releases.

5. *Other media.* This means newspaper journalists in cities where the artists will be appearing, television journalists, and other important journalists who may be covering the recording industry or a specific act.

6. *Concert promoters and bookers.* Since these people have a direct bearing on the personal appearances of the act—which help record sales, media coverage, and income for the act—they need to be made aware of an act's recordings.

Press Kits

The essential tool for publicity is the press kit. The two basic elements for a press kit are a bio (biography) and a picture. The bio is a one- or two-page synopsis of the act containing essential background information; the picture should be a black-and-white glossy. Other elements may include reprints of pertinent reviews and articles, a fact sheet of basic information, more pictures with different poses, a discography, and a copy of the latest recording.

Consumers

The first step toward reaching consumers is the music press. This is the media, generally print, which covers a specific kind of music. For example, there is *Music City News*, *Country Music* and *Country Song Round-Up* for country music; *Downbeat* and *Jazziz* for jazz; *Guitar Player* and *Frets* for guitar players, *Keyboard* for keyboardists, and a number of other publications that appeal to those with an interest in a specific music. These publications are open to new acts as well as established ones and the readers of these publications are active, involved music consumers.

Another key area for consumer awareness is tour publicity. In tour publicity, the publicist contacts local media—newspapers and TV shows—in cities where a performer is appearing or scheduled to appear to encourage a journalist to do an interview, feature story and/or a concert review of the act's show. There is a local angle, so newspaper journalists are generally open to doing a story (especially of a major act). This allows music consumers who are newspaper readers in an area to become aware of a particular act or recording beyond what is heard on radio.

Consumer magazines other than the music press are another vital area for publicizing acts. These broaden the acts' exposure and appeal beyond the core group of fans who read the music press publications. These may include news magazines (such as *Time*, *Newsweek*), men's or women's magazines (*Gentlemen's Quarterly*, *Ladies' Home Journal*), business magazines (*Forbes*, *Business Week*) or magazines aimed at a specific market but which may run a feature on a recording artist if the artist is involved in the activity or interests of the magazine's readers. Examples of the last may include *Runner's World, Men's Health,* or a number of other magazines with a target market. For an artist, the advantage of a feature in these magazines is that it broadens the artist's image and gets them exposure in media not normally available to a recording artist.

National television shows are also important in creating awareness for an act with the decided advantage than an act can receive national coverage with one appearance. These tend to be the most difficult to obtain as well as the most immediately beneficial. Popular national talk shows (both daytime and evening) are good examples, although local TV shows—including newscasts and talk shows—often provide valuable exposure in specific markets.

Publicity Plan

When a publicity plan for an act is developed, goals must first be established; for example, perhaps a certain position on the charts, exposure in specific media—perhaps a certain number of print stories—an awareness of the act by key journalists, exposure in a certain region or city, and sales are all viable objectives for an act. Next, the act must be evaluated to ascertain whether they are articulate, willing and capable of doing interviews, whether they appear attractive on television, and how they handle themselves in tense or awkward situations.

The next step is to determine the appropriate media for the act, matching the objectives of the record label and the attributes of the act. Equally important is where the artist should *not* appear: perhaps a TV talk show is the wrong medium, or perhaps television itself does not work well for the artist. From here the publicity plan and the marketing plan merge and are put into action, hopefully complementing each other.

Publicity and Promotion

Americans generally want to know about successful people—not unknowns. Therefore, there is little demand for a new act with no hit recording. The publicity department will concentrate on print media at the beginning of an artist's career, particularly the trade press, music press, and local media where the artist is appearing. When a single is released, the burden is on the promotion department to deliver a "hit," that is, getting radio to play the recording. When people hear a recording over and over, they are more likely to want to know about the act. This is where publicity comes in and a hit will bring a demand for interviews, stories, and other exposure in the media.

As the hit recording peaks and then descends the charts, the publicist will be busy working to make the act itself a hit so that consumers will want to hear the next release. Thus promotion creates a demand for publicity by promoting hit recordings on radio, then publicity creates a demand for promotion when radio wants to hear more recordings. And if these recordings become hits, consumers want to see and read more about the act, therefore creating a demand for more publicity. It is this effective entwining of the efforts of publicity and promotion that creates more hits and, eventually, artists who are "stars" and do not have to depend upon how well their current recording is doing on radio in order to sell concert tickets or receive exposure in the media. Too, if publicity is effective, it will allow an artist to be exposed in the media even when the act does not have a current single that is a hit, carrying them through slow times in their recording career and hopefully insuring a demand for albums even when there are no major hit singles.

Tools of Publicity: The Bio

The most important tool for the practice of publicity is the bio. This biography is an essential part of any artist's press kit. Its purpose is to introduce an artist, through the printed word, to someone else who knows nothing about him or her, providing some important, factual background information on the artist as well as (hopefully) creating a lasting image. This is done not only by giving basic facts about an artist that others need to know but also by stressing certain aspects about what is appealing about this artist.

A bio is important because it primarily goes to the media, who provide the key link between the artist and the consumer. People in the media write and broadcast articles, columns, features, and other information about artists and recordings. The way the members of the media get their initial information about these artists and recordings is from the record companies, who supply both press kits and copies of recordings to the media in order to obtain exposure.

Compiling bios and press kits is one of the functions of the publicity department of a label. While tour press occupies most of the day-to-day activity of publicity departments, writing a bio is one of the most essential because it is this foundation on which most of the publicity for an artist's career is built.

In compiling a bio, it must be stressed that the bio includes certain basic, factual information. This information may include where and when the artist was born, their basic background (schooling, jobs, etc.), and perhaps what their parents did, if it relates directly to their musical career. It should also include some information about their musical influences and how they came to be signed to a major label or began performing. While certain basic, factual information is important and essential, other information is not. This is because the bio is used as a tool to help "shape" an artist's image.

In discussing "image" it is essential to assert that an image cannot be totally fabricated without any link to the basic, essential nature of the artist. In other words, an image should be based in truth and fact, an extension of what this person is really like. In the long run, a totally fabricated image will not work because the artist will not live up to a false and manufactured image.

Initially, bios are sent to in-house recording company personnel so the entire staff can know about an artist and, hopefully, get behind them in their quest for success in the recording industry. Next, key media—especially print—get these bios, because the artist depends on the media for exposure to consumers. The media will often decide whether to do an article or feature on an artist after reading a bio and being either suitably impressed or strikingly unimpressed.

Booking agents and promoters also need bios and press kits because these help generate bookings, which provide most of the income for a beginning act. Many promoters make decisions about booking a new act partly on the press kit. Also, booking agents can help create interest with promoters for an act with a strong, effective press kit.

Finally, a bio and press kit will be sent to others who may help an artist's career in the long run. These include movie producers, TV show talent directors, those who book artists on commercials, and the international departments of labels, which often determine whether a new act should be developed in an international market.

In general, press kits or bios are reserved for those who are professionally involved in an artist's career. Consumers and fans do not get them and never see them unless the bio is printed verbatim in the media, which sometimes does occur, especially in local newspapers when an artist is on tour.

Press Releases

A press release is news written from a news source and about the source for the news media. It attempts to both inform and influence, presenting the point of view of the company or person generating the story. Press releases are the backbone of publicity.

Since a press release is, essentially, a news story, it must be factual and concise. Although it does represent the point of view of the person or company it is about, it should not be heavy handed or overtly propagandistic in its tone or style but rather should present an accurate, truthful story that contains facts and quotes in a reasonably objective manner. Since a press release represents news from the news source, it does not have to be balanced; that is, it does not have to present both sides of an issue or question and may be selective in the facts it does present. However, it must contain facts and be accurate because the integrity of the source as well as the publicist is dependent on being a service to the media, not an adversary or a source of questionable information.

Publicists working for recording labels generally send out news releases on topics such as the signing of an artist, promotion of an employee, major statements from the company (such as profits for the year or major realignments), the death of an artist, or major awards received by the label and its artists. There may also be releases to counter negative news or correct inaccurate information the media has received.

In addition to the press release that is basically a news release, there are some other kinds of releases used by the recording industry. The *filler* or *blurb* is intended for columnists. These are just small bits of information that are interesting and usually about an artist. Examples would be an incident in the artist's life, upcoming tours, or news about a new release. Finally, a press release may be sent out that is more like a feature than a news story. These, though rarely sent, may be effective because smaller media—local newspapers in smaller towns and small magazines—may run the story as it is.

News Photos

A publicist for a major label will be a source of photos as well as press releases. Although most major daily newspapers have their own photographers, the music trades, the music press, and smaller newspapers do not and thus depend upon publicity departments to supply photos for their publications. Generally, the publicist will hire an independent photographer although sometimes a publicist will be expected to take pictures.

In providing pictures to the media, publicists must remember to make the photo interesting and avoid the five standard clichés in publicity photos: the check pass, the shovel dig, the handshake, the ribbon-cutting and the plaque pass. In sending a picture to the media, the publicist should convey a message or a story.

A professional picture sent to the media will be black and white, generally 8 x 10 with a white border around the picture (so editors can mark them). The publicist should not send out slides, Polaroids, or color prints because they don't reproduce well—all those colors turn to gray when printed in a newspaper or magazine. The black-and-white photo should have good contrast because newspapers especially are printed on cheap, low-quality paper and inferior photos turn to "mud" or just masses of gray and black. The publicist should always try to provide several photos, especially to the most important media, including both a horizontal and vertical shot. This gives editors a choice in case there are space limitations (and there usually are).

The photo caption, or cutline, should be written on a separate sheet of paper, and placed about a third of the way down the paper. The cutline should capture the essence of the story in a sentence or two and all people in the picture should be clearly identified, from left to right. The sheet of paper containing the cutline should be folded over, with the crease coming just above the cutline. The photo should be slipped into the crease facing up, with the cutline sheet on top. The cutline sheet is held in place on the back of the photo with a strip of tape. The recipient easily sees both cutline sheet and the accompanying photo.

Publicity Photos

Publicity photos are used for press kits and to obtain exposure for artists in the media. These are usually posed—although concert shots are also acceptable—and done by a professional photographer.

The publicity photos used in press kits are 8 x 10 black-and-white glossies. Generally, there should be several shots available—a head shot, perhaps a different pose that covers from waist up or the whole person, and vertical as well as horizontal photos. A publicist should also have color slides available on an artist because major publications will sometimes run color shots. Too, when cover stories are run, the label, through the publicist, generally supplies these pictures. Often the label even provides the color separations as well.

Publicity photos are produced in quantity and have the artist's name at the bottom of the picture in a one-inch white strip, as well as the name of the label and perhaps the names of the publicist and booking agent. It is essential that publicity photos be labeled this way for several reasons: (1) attached cutlines may be separated from the picture; (2) publicists often do not have the time to label all photos; and (3) very few artists are instantly recognizable to all those who come into contact with their pictures.

The publicist must keep in mind that, as with the bio, the artist is establishing an image with their photo;

therefore, careful attention should be paid to background, clothes, and poses to insure that a message consistent with the image of the artist is being conveyed by the photograph.

Tour Publicity

Tour publicity involves sending out press kits of an artist to the media in the city or area where the artist will be performing. It also involves scheduling interviews with local media, phoning ahead to alert media of the artist's appearances, and coordinating activities with the promoter of the show involving the commitments and obligations of the artist on the road with regard to his/her relationship with the media.

The publicist usually sends a press kit ahead of the artist's appearance to the media who will do the interview. Sometimes this is done before a phone call from the publicist soliciting an interview so that the writers and editors can become aware of the act and somewhat familiar with them. But the phone call is the essential element that, hopefully, convinces the media to cover the artist with a prominent story and photo.

Artists who are major stars may not want to do stories for each local paper. In this case, the publicist may send color slides and try to convince editors to use these in the paper as well as black-and-white photos. If a press conference is to be scheduled, the publicist must set that up. Otherwise, the paper will craft their own story from the bio and other information in the press kit. The final step is getting copies of the stories run (or "clips") for the artist's file. The best stories may be reprinted and included in the press kit.

For the publicist, tour publicity is the most time-consuming job because it is usually a daily event. For artists, it is essential because it lets them know the label is working for them while they are out on the road—instead of forgotten when they're not in the home office. Too, it helps get people to the concert and, since print is the source of much other media, helps artists stay in the news.

Fame tends to be a cumulative, rather than instantaneous, experience for an artist. It is generally not one big splash somewhere that creates a strong, national following for an act but instead a number of stories in smaller publications, localized to different cities and regions. Too, TV depends on print as a source for most of its news, and the more print media coverage an artist can acquire, the more that major TV shows—as well as national consumer publications—consider the artist worthy for coverage in their publications. Finally, the more "small" interviews an artist does, the better prepared he/she is to do "big" ones, having become comfortable with the interview situation.

In order to generate successful, ongoing publicity that benefits an artist's career, the artist must be articulate, look attractive, not be volatile and explode in touchy or awkward situations. He or she should be able to be depended on to avoid touchy topics, answer pertinent questions, and generally leave a favorable impression. While some artists may be "naturals" at creating strong, positive images for themselves through the media, many other artists must be coached by publicists and put through a "media school" where they are taught the basic skills of effective interviews, including how to answer awkward or touchy questions, how to always present their best side to the media and make the necessary points regardless of what the interviewer asks, and how to control an interview by answering statements from interviewers, steering the interview to the subjects the artist is most comfortable with, and providing transitions during the conversation that will keep the interview focused on the artist and his/her work.

Media Buys

The primary function of the advertising department for a recording label is placing media buys. This means purchasing advertising space in the media and contrasts with the primary function of publicity, which is getting media exposure for an act without placing media buys. Obviously, it is necessary for both publicity and advertising to work together for maximum effective exposure.

To successfully market a recording artist, the effective use of a variety of media is essential. This is called the *media mix* and entails determining which media should be used for maximum exposure to the predetermined audience in the marketing plan. But before this mix can be discussed, it is necessary to examine all the media available to a record company, outlining the pros and cons of each medium.

Radio

The most important media for a recording act is the radio; here is where the exposure of an artist's recordings leads directly to sale of the artist's recorded product and a corresponding demand for an artist's appearances. Since the recording industry is both business and entertainment (like sports), each recording played on radio, in essence, constitutes an advertisement. However, recording labels sometimes want to supplement airplay—or perhaps create airplay—for a recording with paid advertising in order to spur sales at the retail level.

In purchasing advertising on radio, the recording label must consider advantages and disadvantages of this medium for advertising. In analyzing radio in this light, the major advantages for purchasing advertising are these:

1. Radio reaches the key buyers of recorded music because most buyers of recordings listen to radio.

2. Radio is the most accessible and inescapable medium—in homes, cars, available while we walk or jog,

inside or outside the home—with an average of five to six radios belonging to each household.

3. It is possible to target an audience through station formats. In other words, if you want to reach a country audience, use a country music station, or an R & B music station for an R & B audience. Further, each station appeals to a specific demographic group: 10 to 19, or 25 to 50, or mostly female, or mostly black.

4. People can hear the act. Most people will not buy a recording unless they have heard it first, and the most likely place to hear a recording is radio. Since each play of a recording is an advertisement for the act, in time buys, portions of the recording may be played.

5. For the 13- to 18-year-old, radio is a way of life. More than any other age group, this demographic group considers radio as a very personal medium, part of their life style and social activities.

6. For the college student, it is an art form as well as a way of life. For that reason, college radio is generally more esoteric as well as adventuresome and accessible to new music and new acts. While mainstream radio tries to find a consistent sound for 24 hours a day, seven days a week, the college radio station will challenge its listeners, perhaps playing a heavy metal number, followed by a German polka band, followed by a big band record, and then a country music number from 1949—and the audience accepts it.

7. Generally there is quick response to a radio ad; for example, an impact on sales will be felt quickly if radio advertising is effective.

8. With time buys, radio is less expensive overall than television.

The disadvantages of time buys for prerecorded product on radio are as follows:

1. It is perishable. If someone is not listening to radio at the time the advertisement is run, they will not hear it. This

is particularly applicable if the advertisement is run during non-peak listening times.

2. A major problem in choosing a particular station in the market for time buys is the number of pop/rock, country, or adult contemporary stations in a major market: if one is selected for ad buys, the others may retaliate by taking the advertiser's record off the air. Then the label is in the situation of having to spend advertising money for radio on stations that are considered nonessential in order to keep the record on the air. This is particularly troubling when there are several very influential stations in a market. Generally, the time buys go to the reporting stations, though another station may be as influential in terms of sales for that particular market.

3. With time buys for prerecorded product, if a station is not regularly playing the recording, the ads probably won't work.

4. Radio is expensive. The disadvantage of time buys in *all* the media is that they can be expensive, especially if a national campaign is being mounted.

Television

In discussing advertising for recorded product on television, the major advantages are these:

1. TV reaches the largest number of people. This is true of the networks as well as local stations in a market. TV is an integral part of American life and the great majority of Americans watch it.

2. TV is visual as well as aural. This is especially important when dealing with acts whose visual appeal is as strong as their recordings.

3. With TV packages, there is an immediate, direct response, primarily through 800 long-distance numbers, credit card orders, and overnight delivery. For these reasons, TV shopping has encouraged impulse buying.

4. TV ads have the lowest cost per person. Since there are so many people in the TV audience, the cost of the ad divided by the number of viewers shows that advertisers are paying less than they would in most other media to reach each individual.

The major disadvantages of purchasing advertising time for prerecorded product on television are these:

1. It is perishable. If someone is not watching at the time the ad is on, they've missed it. Further, with channel surfing and video tapes—where viewers fast-forward during the commercials—it is possible viewers will miss the ad; indeed, much of TV's technology is used by viewers in order to avoid the advertisements.

2. As an advertising medium, TV is most expensive overall for a national campaign.

3. With TV advertising, it is extremely difficult to target the market. Although this has changed with the advent of cable channels (particularly ESPN, MTV, and the Nashville Network), television generally does not allow an advertiser to target those with specific tastes in music. In other words, people watching a popular show may like rock or bluegrass or classical or any other kind of music—and there is no way to separate them. Thus an advertisement will reach a lot of people who have no interest in your product and will never buy it.

4. TV is not very cost efficient in breaking new acts because audiences tend to buy someone with name recognition or something they've heard before.

Print

It is a little more difficult to discuss print media because there are so many more aspects: there are local newspapers, national magazines, the music press, music industry trade magazines, and even billboards. However, to speak in the most general terms possible, the advantages of buying advertisements for prerecorded product in the print media are these:

1. It transcends time. If someone doesn't have the time to read something now, it will wait. And, unlike radio and television, it can be passed along to others.

2. With print media buys for prerecorded product, it is possible to target the market very well. This applies especially to local publications, such as newspapers, when attempting to reach a specific market, as well as specialty publications, like the music press, where the audience is known to be interested in music—and usually a specific *kind* of music.

3. With advertisement purchases in the print media, it is possible to establish a visual image for an artist. Since an artist's looks are as important as their music in a long-term career, it is essential a visual image be established, and print does that best.

4. As a rule, print tends to be more personal. At the local level, readers usually feel a closeness to the publication.

5. Advertising buys in the print media generally cost less overall for a national campaign where one advertisement in a print publication can reach a national audience. This contrasts with a number of local buys on radio or the cost of network advertising on television, both of which cost a great deal more.

6. With media buys for prerecorded product in the print media, a label can work tie-ins with local record stores. This applies primarily to newspaper advertisements and allows for co-op money to be available for advertising, lowering the cost the label has to spend. (In co-op advertising the label and the retailer each pay a portion.) Print advertisements also work well with in-store appearances by acts as do concert promotions.

7. Print advertisements for prerecorded product work well with multiproduct formats. No reader is turned off to

see a classical album pictured with a rock release and a country album in a print ad. This allows a record company to receive exposure with ad buys for a number of acts on its roster and contrasts with radio or TV where one type of music—and usually only one or two acts—may receive exposure from each advertisement.

8. With print media, the over-25 consumer trusts and responds. As individuals get older, they are more likely to read and less likely to spend as much time with radio because of job demands as well as a maturing process that has them seeking information in a variety of media as well as entertainment.

The major disadvantages of purchasing advertisements for prerecorded product in the print media are as follows:

1. There is generally a poor to fair response with young buyers and the college age audience for the print media. Simply put, this audience listens to the electronic media more than they read print; therefore it is harder to reach these active buyers of recorded product through print.

2. With print media, it is not possible to hear the artist, which is really the *major* disadvantage of print media, because the vast majority of buyers will not buy an act they have never heard.

3. Print advertising for prerecorded product has the highest cost per person. Although advertisers reach the target market better, they will pay a higher cost per person simply because they are not reaching as many or are generally not reaching those peripherally interested.

4. The reproduction quality in newspapers is poor for advertisements. The paper used in newspapers is cheap, hence ads will generally not look as attractive; this could be crucial if a label is working to provide a visual image for an act.

In addition to these mediums of radio, television, and print, there are several other areas where record companies must decide whether or not to spend money. These include videos, in-store promotions, and consumer contests.

Videos are generally not viewed as advertising expenses; however, in determining how to effectively spend money to market an act, videos must be considered. The primary role of videos is to serve as a supplement to radio, "watching radio," as it were. But videos are increasingly used in ways outside video clips for TV. They are also used in sales meetings, as part of a press kit, for booking agents, and even for auditions for movie and TV roles. In discussing the expenditure of money for videos a label must consider several key factors.

The advantages of using videos as a marketing tool for prerecorded product are these:

1. Videos, like TV, are visual as well as aural, allowing a consumer to *see* as well as *hear* an act. The appeal of an attractive act may be showcased effectively with video.

2. Uses for video are growing. Even if the video is not aired on TV, it may be used with in-store promotions, as part of a video-biography, for use internationally, and on television shows (such as news) when the artist is unavailable.

3. Video serves as another alternative to radio, which means another opportunity for an act to get exposure outside the traditional outlet of radio.

4. Video is an excellent way to establish a visual image for an act, especially through concept videos. Further, this image can extend beyond the "looks" of an act to include issues, interests, and activities that help define an act.

5. Music videos are "contemporary," another way of saying that they are perceived as "in" and a necessity for both acts and audiences.

The disadvantages of spending money on videos in order to market prerecorded product are as follows:

1. Videos can be *very* expensive, sometimes costing more than an entire album. Thus, an even greater number of record sales are necessary in order for the recording label to recoup its investment.

2. There are not many ways for a label to recoup the costs of a video other than album sales. Granted, some artists have generated significant sales with their videos, and some consumers have expressed a willingness to purchase music videos; however, for most acts, video sales are simply not that significant—the primary reason for a video remains to generate sales of prerecorded product.

3. Effective outlets for music video are limited in number. "Effective" means that the airing of a video is directly related to immediate, significant sales of an artist's recorded product. A video on MTV in high rotation will certainly generate sales for some rock acts, and the Nashville Network and CMT have proven effective for some country acts, but the fact remains that outlets other than these are not nearly as powerful or effective.

Another consideration when spending money to market an act's recording is in-store promotion, which generally takes the form of point-of-purchase material. These materials are posters, mobiles, stand-ups, banners, and anything else that can be displayed in a store. These materials are for display purposes only, *not* merchandising at concerts. The advantages for the label of supplying point-of-purchase material to retailers are:

1. This material reaches consumers when they are in a place to make a purchase.

2. The material helps establish a visual image of the act.

The disadvantages of a label supplying POP material to retailers are:

1. This material is hard to control; there is no guarantee the store personnel will use this material.

2. POP material can be quite expensive. If several posters, flats, stand-ups and whatever else are sent to each store for a campaign, the cost can add up quickly.

To help insure that POP material will be put on display in stores, labels often use in-store contests. These contests are aimed at store personnel, who are usually awarded prizes for the best display. The public will never know about these contests because they are between the labels and the stores. The advantages of labels sponsoring in-store contests are:

1. These contests help insure the POP material gets displayed.

2. The contests reward key retail personnel. If they do a good job, retail salespeople may help a label sell a number of albums—and they should be rewarded.

3. In-store contests get retail personnel involved with the label's artist and product. Obviously, when retail salespeople feel involved in an act, they will do a better job in trying to sell product from that act.

The disadvantages of a label sponsoring in-store contests are these:

1. They are expensive. Costs of prizes and materials can add up quickly.

2. There are the problems of administrating the contest. Usually someone at the label has to take the time to judge the contest, make sure the prizes arrive and, if something is broken, have it fixed. This person is usually a local promotion person who has a number of other things to do for the label.

3. The in-store contest may not work. Perhaps the act is not appealing, or the record is not a hit, or the prizes don't catch the fancy of the personnel; at any rate, it is possible that store personnel will choose not to be involved in a label's POP material, even when there is a contest. There is also the possibility (and this has happened!) that the store

personnel will put up a display after-hours, take a photo for the contest, then immediately dismantle the display, so the label gets no benefits because consumers never see it.

The contests consumers know about are called consumer contests and are usually done in conjunction with a radio station. The prizes usually involve a trip to see the act or free albums and T-shirts. The advantages of these consumer contests are these:

1. They get consumers involved with the act. Usually the contest involves calling a local radio station, answering a question about the act, or knowing something about their product.

2. They create excitement at the consumer level, especially true when the prize involves a trip or meeting the act.

3. With a consumer contest, the label can tie in their efforts with local stores and stations. This enables a label to maintain good relations with key radio and retail personnel.

The disadvantages of consumer contests sponsored by labels are as follows:

1. There is a small payoff. A consumer will usually buy only one album, although the publicity generated by the contest may be beneficial in the long run.

2. Again, there is the problem of administrating the contest. The burden usually falls to the recording label, where someone must find the time to do this in addition to regular duties.

Help from Independents

In discussing how a record company should spend its money marketing product, several other options should be considered. These include hiring independent promotion and independent publicity firms, which is akin to other types of companies hiring outside consultants. Outside firms are advantageous when they support the efforts of the label, giving added expertise and that is the major advantage. But the disadvantages are that an outside firm may be difficult to control and they add another layer of expense to the budget.

The issue of whether a label should hire independent promotion people has gone through several cycles. Originally, the labels thought they could do the job themselves best and looked at the indies as a distraction. As the indies were hired by managers, artists, publishing companies, and others, and proved to be effective, the labels came to view them as perhaps a necessary evil and then a vital, helpful part of the music industry. When sales slowed in the 1970s and a number of label promotion people were dismissed, they often set up their own independent companies. The labels realized they still needed the help of these promotion people but liked hiring them independently because the constant overhead of salaries and benefits did not have to be paid.

However, in the mid-1980s a payola scandal in rock music erupted as the competition between indies led them to unsavory business practices to keep what they felt to be a competitive edge. As the indies got more powerful, the labels felt they were being blackmailed—huge sums were being extracted in order to get records played on specific stations and the labels felt helpless to change the situation. Eventually, this led to a general policy from major labels to not hire any independent promotion people.

Gradually, several changes occurred. First, labels began hiring a number of indies to be staff people again—keeping their promotional efforts at a competitive level while being able to control the promotion. Next, labels began to again hire independent promotion people on a more selective basis, avoiding agreements where a label had to pay in order for each reporting station to go on a record.

8

Independent Labels and Specialty Music

When people refer to the "music industry" or "music business," they are generally referring to one aspect—the corporate powers like WEA, Sony, BMG/RCA, MCA, Capitol/EMI and Polygram that dominate the world of mainstream commercial music, reflected by the music industry's trade charts. These corporations dominate the worlds of pop/rock music, country music, and R & B, or urban music, with their distribution, sales, promotion, and marketing networks. But they generally do not create the musical trends nor do they dominate music outside the mainstream. Here, the independent labels are the essence of the music industry.

Anyone can start a recording label; as the old saying goes, all you need is a checkbook and a phone book. It takes some capital, obviously, and it takes some artists and recordings. The independent label represents small business at its best and most innovative—the true entrepreneurial spirit of the recording industry. The indie will operate much like the majors—they will take the artist's recordings, ship singles to radio stations, try to get the stations to play them, and try to get stores to stock the product by using independent distributors. The independent distribution system is a key difference. These independent distributors will take product from a number of smaller labels and get them to the stores.

An independent label will have to deal with a number of these independent distributors, located in a number of major cities, to get distribution for their product. This contrasts with the major labels who have their own in-house distribution system. The alternative is for a small label to be distributed by a major label; this usually occurs when someone within the industry who has "clout" decides to start their own label and uses the major label's manufacturing and distribution networks to get the recordings in the marketplace. In this latter case, the small label is almost an extension of the major label except the small label owns the copyright. Another alternative is for a major label to own a portion of an independent label, buy into an independent distribution system (or create an indie system for small labels), or spin off small labels under the corporate umbrella.

Most independent labels do not attempt to compete with the major labels by having a large roster of artists doing pop/rock, country, and R & B music. Instead, small independent labels either concentrate their efforts regionally or specialize in a certain kind of music, or "specialty music." Specialty music is nonmainstream music and includes classical, jazz, gospel, children's, folk, bluegrass, blues, Cajun, ethnic, and other kinds of music. The major labels generally do not release product on these specialty musics because (1) they feel the markets are too small; (2) they don't have the expertise or interest at the executive level to market these specialty musics effectively; and (3) it would take a special effort to develop each of these markets, requiring the hiring of additional people and spending time nurturing their growth. Projected sales would probably not be enough to warrant these efforts; hence, it would not be profitable so the major labels do not bother.

This means that a lot of music falls between the cracks. On one hand, there are consumers in the marketplace wanting to purchase different kinds of music. On the other hand, there aren't *enough* consumers that can be reached through mainstream radio or retail to entice the major labels to pursue these consumers. This is where the independent labels fit into the picture.

Independent labels dominate the fields of gospel, jazz, folk, bluegrass, classical, spoken word, children's, and various ethnic musics. The independents know these markets, work them well, and learn how to market in areas and in ways the major labels either don't know about and/or don't care to pursue. The major recording labels do an excellent job of what they do best: getting mainstream music exposure and sales in mainstream outlets. What they *don't* do well is market a variety of smaller musics in the nonmainstream outlets.

The major labels tend to be marketing organizations who have as their main product musical recordings. The independent labels tend to be music organizations who must use marketing to get their music exposed to interested consumers. The major labels try to have something for everyone; the smaller labels have what a relative handful want. Independent labels can be profitable ventures, but not on the scale of a multimillion-dollar global firm, which is the level where the major labels operate. Still, for many, independent labels fulfill the passion for music so many music executives feel while, at the same time, they provide a competitive product in the market-based music economy.

The most essential difference between the independent labels who market specialty music and the major recording labels for exposing their respective musics is the major media outlets. For the major labels, airplay on mainstream radio is how most music is exposed and where audiences connect with the music; for specialty music, it is print media and college or alternative radio that are the major ways in which the label reaches consumers. Print media may take the form of music press periodicals targeted to this market, newsletters generated in-house and sent to a core of consumers, or catalogs where consumers may order this specialty music. With major labels, mainstream radio dominates the marketing, followed by television and then print. With specialty music, the order is reversed, with print dominating marketing, followed by television and, finally mainstream radio. While alternative radio—especially college radio or public radio—plays a key role in the exposure and marketing of some specialty musics, it is difficult if not impossible to depend heavily on any type of radio with nonmainstream music. Still, the key to hits in specialty music usually requires some kind of radio airplay, especially in the fields of alternative, gospel, bluegrass, and folk music. College radio, with its adventuresome programming, has been especially important in breaking new ground as well as new acts and new music. Indeed, college radio is probably *the* single most important medium in marketing specialty musics, while mainstream radio is nearly insignificant.

Classical Music

It is unfair to lump a wide variety of music that includes symphonies, string quartets, single instrument performers, opera, vocalists, romantic composers, minimalist composers, and many others under "classical," but it is done. While each of these musics has its adherents, and these adherents defend their turf vociferously, there are some common elements in what has become known as the "classical" audience. First, this audience tends to be well educated, very literate, and mostly affluent. They appreciate classical music as much for its heritage as for its contemporary appeal.

Major recording labels generally have classical divisions, although most are not major money makers. However, the labels generally feel that classical music is important, part of their musical heritage, and they continue to carry it out of a sense of duty as well as a hope for profit. Classical music has an audience of cultured, sophisticated listeners and many of those in the top executive positions at major labels want to find favor with this audience.

Historically, classical music—particularly opera—played a major role in the development of the major recording labels, especially Victor, which later became RCA. The most profitable early recordings were often of opera performers and the first buyers of the new technology of recorded sound in the late nineteenth and early twentieth century were often classical buyers. Indeed, the first international recording "star" was Enrico Caruso, an opera performer. However, after World War II classical music dropped from 18 to approximately 5 percent of recorded music sold.

Classical music has long served as the best way to present new recording technology to the public. When the long-playing record was presented to the public by Columbia in 1948, the impetus for its development over the 78 rpm format was that classical recordings could be more easily recorded and presented in this format. And when the compact disc technology was marketed in the 1980s, the first market targeted was the classical market. There are some reasons for this: (1) the classical music buyer tends to be more affluent and thus able to afford new technology; (2) there tend to be more audiophiles among classical listeners; and (3) since classical music buyers tend to be more literate, it is easier to reach them through the print media and present the reasons for new technology to them in meaningful ways. But there are other reasons as well, especially in the shift to the compact disc in the 1980s.

Basically, all of the "classics" have been recorded. Conductors and soloists who continue to record the classics by Beethoven, Mozart, Mahler, and others, pull from this same pool, hoping to appeal to their audience with a "new" or "different" interpretation of the work or by "star" appeal. But despite the fact there are some composers continuing to compose "classical" works, or works in the "classical" tradition, the fact remains that the majority of this repertoire has already been done a number of times.

Labels have managed to sell classical recordings by creating a "line" of product (e.g., the complete symphonies of Beethoven, or the complete operas of Mozart) and in their catalog they have a large selection of recordings already done. Since the original production of these recordings has been paid, the only cost is in repackaging and thus it is easier to make a profit. Still, it has been technology that has offered the major breakthroughs for this music, and consumers have found the technology the "newest" aspect of this music, especially if this technology can enhance the sound of the recordings and provide a setting where a whole work can be heard as it was composed.

The live concert appearance is still the major medium for classical artists. The recordings that give the most lifelike sound reproduction of live concerts are therefore most successful. From the standpoint of publicity and promotion, these live performances are the means by which the classical artist reaches critics, who generally write in the print media, giving the artist broad exposure. While there is some exposure on public radio and public television for contemporary classical artists, the mass medium that is most important is print. Print exposure is most likely to be obtained from live performances.

Yet, although live performances are the lifeblood of classical music, the audience for symphony concerts has generally declined through the years. Thus there are "pops" concerts (featuring classical and popular songs by symphonies), guest celebrity artists from other fields of music, and other special programs, offerings and gimmicks to attract regular listeners to classical concerts.

There are various reasons for the decline of the classical listening audience; some of them are increased competition from other forms of entertainment, the high quality of recordings now on the market, the fact that recordings of favorite composers and works are on the market, and that the music has generally failed to regenerate itself, providing new exciting performers, composers or works that the public wants to see.

Classical music is sold in regular retail outlets, in independent stores, megastores, by direct mail, through record clubs (which increasingly specialize in music for their audience) and catalogs. It is a music with a continuing appeal in a country where history and heritage are less important than the sounds of the moment. And it will continue to have an audience, albeit a relatively small one compared to the rest of the music industry. This small audience (roughly 5 percent of total music sold) will attract new buyers generally from the college audience, which is more open as well as educated and thus appreciative of classical music, and from those who find that a taste for classical is part of a larger self-image of being cultured and refined in the worlds of art, literature, and music. The biggest problem for classical music is gaining new audiences to add to the existing base and making classical music competitive in a market economy. Generally, classical music needs the support of arts organizations and outside funding in order to survive.

Jazz

Like classical music, a number of different types of music are linked under the name "jazz." The roots of jazz go back to New Orleans and a sound described today as Dixieland. Today jazz includes such sounds as this traditional music, bebop from the post-World War II music of Charlie "Bird" Parker and Dizzy Gillespie, "cool" jazz led by Miles Davis from the 1950s, experimental jazz, New Age music, fusion jazz, some instrumental music, and contemporary or improvisational jazz.

Jazz is appealing to young pop buyers, particularly fusion or other kinds with a pop production. For these people, jazz is an instrumental music—R & B music or pop sounds without lyrics. For some who call themselves true jazz fans, this is not really jazz at all. The same may be said for New Age jazz, also called Yuppie Muzak by those who do not favor these sounds. New Age music is more chordal than melodic and sometimes seems to seek "sounds" that are pleasing rather than musicianship that is avant-garde, experimental, or exciting. Still, New Age jazz has given the jazz field a shot in the arm, accounting for large sales. Significantly, these sales began in bookstores, from in-store airplay in record stores, and from live performances rather than from radio, the traditional medium for exposing music.

New Age jazz has created a definable sound—no matter what instrument is featured—as well as album cover art that lets consumers define the music inside without first hearing it. It seems to offer listeners a music that is soothing in a hectic world and fulfills an important function: relaxing the mind and ears of listeners.

Others would argue that jazz should excite the mind and ears of listeners, and these fans want a music that challenges listeners. These fans are more likely to fit the self-image of this music: a musically elite group who are aware of great music and great musicians simply by hearing it on record. This provides an interesting contrast to the pop music world, which is heavily into stardom and the star system. For the jazz fan, the music itself is the "star."

Jazz is generally well accepted in record stores and receives a significant amount of in-store airplay, providing a nice balance between the young rock fans and the older fans who are more likely to be fans of softer sounds because jazz is generally acceptable to them both. There is limited exposure on radio and television, although public stations generally include some jazz programming. The major media exposure comes from print, usually generated from live performances.

Jazz is a music geared especially to live performances, for musicians improvising and "playing off" one another so that each performance is different from every other one, even when the same songs are played. There are a number of jazz festivals in this country, which attract a large lineup of jazz performers. The college audience is generally open to jazz and colleges regularly book jazz performers for concerts, and college radio usually provides some jazz programming.

Dance Music

Dance music is for clubs where people socialize, party, and (obviously!) dance. It is characterized by a strong beat and is usually longer than the traditional three-minute hit because people want to dance longer than that. This music is usually played over expensive, elaborate sound systems and the club disc jockey plays a key role. He or she picks the records, based on what mood is being created and which recordings work best with getting people out on the dance floor, and often creates his or her own sounds from these recordings—turning off the vocal, spotlighting the bass, and other activities to excite dancers.

While dance music is part of mainstream music—mainly part of the R&B music division—it is also a specialty music. Small independent labels find acts and promote them at local clubs. Since the promotion of these recordings is dependent on getting disc jockeys in local clubs to play the recordings, and not dependent on radio airplay, there is a personal contact and feedback often missing in mainstream music. When a dance record is playing, the disc jockey can see immediately how people are accepting or rejecting it. At retail, dance music has been largely responsible for the creation of the market for the extended play song.

Rap

If there is a modern example of a specialty music that began on small, independent labels and then, through public acceptance, entered the mainstream (and major recording labels) it is rap. Rap is an urban folk music, coming from black disc jockeys with their jive talk as well as inner city black youth whose verbal word play brought a poetry into their own lifes to tell of their hopes, dreams, and frustrations, as well as daily life in the 'hood. Rap is also the classic story of a music that started small, recorded and released by small, independent labels, until it caught on with a larger market when the major recording labels took notice. Major labels bought the small labels or worked out distribution agreements with them; they also signed rap artists to the major labels.

In the beginning, rap was sold in (mostly) independent stores in the inner city to black youth; as it became more popular, and was distributed by major labels, it became widely available in mainstream outlets and the major buyers became young white males. Originally, live performances and word of mouth were used to market this music; as it became more popular, radio and TV exposure became available.

Alternative Music and Heavy Metal

Alternative music is an offshoot of mainstream music and part of its image is that it is noncommercial. The term "alternative" encompasses a wide variety of music—heavy metal, hard rock, grunge, and death rock all fall under the general heading of alternative. Because the emphasis is on the message that this is not a music for the middle class, many alternative music acts have been reluctant to join major recording labels. Independent labels that are regionally based (Seattle is a good example with its grunge bands) have dominated this music and the major media outlet is college radio.

Alternative music groups generally develop a local following by playing clubs and their sales of recordings on independent labels are dependent upon someone with the small label keeping in constant touch with local record stores, local radio, and other local media outlets. Although successful acts can develop a national following, the core following for alternative music is local or regional in scope.

Heavy metal music has traditionally appealed to young male fans and has been marketed through visual appeal—most of the bands are highly theatrical and seek to present a "look" that is readily identifiable as heavy metal—and through extensive touring. Most heavy metal bands build a following through constant personal appearances; radio exposure is limited but TV, via video clips, has proven more open to heavy metal.

Independent labels have always dominated heavy metal with a number of labels distributed by major labels. Significant sales in the gold and platinum range are possible, but most groups do not achieve sales at this level.

Gospel

Gospel is unique because, although it is part of the music industry—making recordings, getting airplay, etc.—its performers' self-image is very different from that of others in the music industry. While most other performers in other kinds of music view themselves as entertainers, or musicians, or performers, or even "artists," the gospel music performer views himself or herself as a minister. For other performers, the music comes first and foremost; for the gospel performer, music is secondary to the ministry: saving souls, instructing, encouraging, and supporting Christian believers, and presenting the Christian message to the public.

The world of gospel music is unique because it has its own marketing network. The Christian bookstore is the primary retail outlet and 90 percent of contemporary Christian product is sold there. Too, there are Christian radio stations that play only Christian recordings, Christian television stations and networks, Christian periodicals, and a Christian booking network that involves a number of churches as well as other venues where Christian acts perform. Indeed, it is quite possible for a performer to be a major star in gospel music while the rest of the music industry is not even aware of this artist.

Gospel music covers a wide variety of musics and the term "gospel" is often misleading because it represents a number of different connotations to different people. First, gospel music, like American Christianity, is divided into black and white markets. While some performers may mix audiences—blacks playing before white audiences or vice versa as well as black and white performers influencing each other—the audiences basically remain segregated. In this field, the term "crossover" generally means a black gospel artist playing for a white gospel audience or a white gospel performer capable of attracting a black gospel audience. However, most gospel music performances consist of white Christian performers playing before white Christian audiences and black Christian performers playing before black Christian audiences.

In white gospel music there are basically three kinds: southern gospel, inspirational, and contemporary Christian music. Southern gospel is the music roughly akin to country music. It is dominated by the "quartet sound" and has its heritage in the shaped note singing developed from singing schools in the South in the nineteenth century. The major event of the year for this group is the National Quartet Convention. This kind of music is generally sold in regular retail outlets—not Christian bookstores—and it often appeals to the country consumer.

It may be argued that all gospel music is "inspirational" so, in a sense, it is a misnomer to categorize one particular type as "inspirational." But the inspiration type of gospel music in the white field is that directed to the church audience. Here are hymns, praise songs, and worship songs geared to the church choir and church congregations on Sunday morning. It is by nature conservative and includes the works of such classic writers as Isaac Watts and the Wesleys as well as new material being written and produced. The function of this music is to edify, instruct, and encourage the Christian churchgoer. Its role in the service is usually to begin the service and "prepare the listener" for the sermon as well as provide musical interludes for the communion service, altar calls, or other parts of the service.

Contemporary Christian music covers all kinds of music not included in the previous two categories. Basically, any kind of secular music you can name has a Christian counterpart. The Christian version copies the musical styles of the secular performers but differs in lyrical content. In fact, it may be argued here that there is no such thing as gospel "music" but there are definitely gospel "songs." There are Christian performers doing heavy metal, hard rock, soft rock, country-rock, folk-rock, middle-of-the-road, jazz, easy listening, pop and any every other kind of commercial music. The rationale of copying secular music is that, in order to attract new believers, you must first give audiences a taste of what they already know. Thus, a heavy metal fan will be inclined to listen to Christian heavy metal music and, through hearing the gospel message in the lyrics, be convinced and converted to Christianity. There is also the notion of "entertainment for the saints." In other words,

Christians want entertainment but want that entertainment to contain the message in the lyrics congruent with their own beliefs. Hence, Contemporary Christian music.

In black gospel there are basically two different kinds of music: traditional and contemporary. Traditional music is based on the black gospel choir, usually a large group who sing in the church. There are soloists for different numbers, but they are all supported by the choir sound. Recordings here are usually done "live" during a church service and reflect the role of gospel music in the black church—a role that includes inspiring, uplifting, encouraging, and supporting the black churchgoer.

The other kind of black gospel—contemporary—is basically a gospel version of urban music heard on black radio. This kind of music is usually recorded in studios and, like R & B music, features groups as well as single acts. It is a music whose role generally lies outside the church service, in a concert setting, or special program, or for those who want their entertainment to fit their religious beliefs, hence Christian lyrics. Black gospel is usually sold in regular retail outlets located in the black sections of a city or town or in stores that have a large black clientele.

Radio is more limited for black gospel performers than it is for white gospel performers. Most black gospel music is heard on programs on black stations. These are Sunday morning programs as well as other regularly scheduled programs with a sponsor to cover the cost. There are very few all-black gospel stations. Black gospel does not have the television or print outlets white gospel does, either. Exposure here is limited and the black gospel performer generally must rely on public performances over a long period of time in order to create a following, although some "hits" do emerge on radio.

In white gospel, particularly in the inspirational and contemporary Christian markets, the major outlet is the

Christian bookstore. These stores sell books, Bibles, sheet music for choirs, jewelry, gift items, and other assorted paraphernalia as well as recorded music. It has been estimated that only about 5 percent of those who call themselves Christians in this country actively shop at these stores, but these are the committed consumers of Christian products. For these people, religion is a vital, important part of their life and their consumer habits reflect this: they listen to Christian radio, watch Christian television programs, read Christian books and periodicals, attend Christian concerts, send their children to Christian schools, are active in Christian organizations (and may even work in a Christian business or organization) and buy Christian music albums. These people want a religious experience when they listen to music and Christian music provides this.

Since this market is geared strongly to and for the Christian, Christian gatekeepers generally censor material and artists who are not decidedly Christian. Here, Christian bookstores feel they are providing a service to their customers by finding out the beliefs of individual artists, authors, and other celebrities, and keeping those whom they consider non-Christian off the shelves. Thus, the Christian consumer trusts the store to not only provide Christian product but also to determine what is "truly Christian" and what is not. For these reasons, it is extremely difficult—if not impossible—for a major secular label to be stocked in a Christian bookstore, or for a gospel album recorded by a secular artist to receive any shelf space in a Christian bookstore.

Since the marketing network is limited to the Christian culture, and since that culture's media does not permeate the secular culture, the Christian marketer must rely on in-store exposure—such as point-of-purchase material (posters, mobiles, and other material) to make Christian consumers aware of new material. The print media is important because of the limits of Christian radio and Christian television.

Christian radio accounts for approximately 2 percent of total radio in this country. Most of these stations are ostensibly commercial, but do not receive much income from commercial advertising. The way they make money is from selling block programming time, or "preaching and teaching" programs to a number of ministers who buy 15-, 30-, and 60-minute blocks of time to deliver their message, followed generally by an appeal for money. If people respond financially, then these programs may buy additional time to stay on the air, perpetuating themselves.

The significance of this block programming in music is that it limits the amount of music that can be programmed. Since there are almost no all-music stations in Christian radio, the audience—which usually prefers music—is limited too. And the audiences who do tune in—the ones who like and support the block programming programs—are generally small, loyal, and adamantly against losing their favorite program or programming more music or even some adventurous music. Again, it is the notion that those in the Christian music industry, in this case radio, are involved in a *ministry* and not entertainment or radio in the traditional, secular sense.

Christian television is limited for musical performers because most of the televangelists who have their own program want to totally control the content, including the musical acts and selections. Thus, most have in-house musical acts and seldom if ever book outside musical performers. While there is *some* exposure for Christian acts for television, it is much lower than would be expected considering the overall amount of Christian programming on television.

The Christian world also provides a network of bookings and venues, primarily through churches. Large churches have budgets for the youth minister and music minister and some of this is earmarked for bringing in recording acts. There are a number of large churches that can not only afford to do this but also attract a large audience to their facilities. There are also a number of Christian colleges with budgets to bring in Christian musical performers. These offer a large audience of like-minded believers and provide an excellent forum for performances as well as a good market for sales of recordings.

The Christian periodicals provide an excellent outlet for information on celebrities in the Christian culture—preachers, teachers, authors, and recording artists. There are a large number of periodicals, organized basically under the Evangelical Press Association, and they permeate this culture probably better than any other media.

The Christian culture is not just interested in the product, whether it is a hit recording or not, but they are more interested in what the performer believes. If performers have the correct "beliefs" or doctrine, they are allowed some leeway in what they present. However, if the person does not possess what is perceived to be the "correct" faith, it does not matter what he or she says or how good the product—he or she will not be accepted.

This is a very conservative culture—politically, socially, musically, and with their faith. These are "careful" people—careful of what they do and say, what images they present to other believers, what other believers should be exposed to, and what they will accept from other believers, and careful to screen anyone in the public eye concerning their faith.

The financial backbone for Christian music is in publishing, specifically publishing for the church. If there is a song popular with choirs—or a popular musical—then enough copies will be bought for each member of the choir as well as the accompanist(s). This may result in significant sales for sheet music. Too, if a song is accepted in a widely circulated songbook or hymnal, significant sales will also result. Thus, publishing is the most lucrative field in gospel music.

The major organization representing the Christian bookstores is the Christian Booksellers Association, which hold an annual convention where orders are placed for recordings, books, and other items stocked in these Christian bookstores.

Children's Music

Since the early 1950s (following the introduction of the 45 rpm record) children's music has been a significant part of the music industry. Targeted primarily to the children nine and under, this music provides entertainment for children as well as teaching them that prerecorded music is an important form of entertainment. In the long term, so the theory goes, this introduction to musical consumerism will entice them to become buyers of prerecorded music when they get older and, when they become parents, buy music for their own children. In short, the success of children's music assures the market that there will be lifelong buyers of prerecorded music because the habit of buying music for the home will be imbedded from earliest childhood.

The baby boom after World War II provided the first large audience for children's music. Manufacturers responded by producing recordings for this market, wrapped in brightly colored covers. Later, as these baby boomers were booming with babies of their own, there was another great wave of buyers of prerecorded music.

Most children's music is sold in mass merchandisers because this is where parents shop most often. The growth of toy stores has provided another strong market for children's music. Record stores, on the other hand, will sometimes stock some children's music but the major sales remain with the rack accounts. Rack jobbers estimate that 15 to 20 percent of their business is children's music.

There are five major advantages to marketing children's music:

1. *High profit margins.* Since production costs are generally lower than those of mainstream music, and since a "classic" recording can last years, there can be greater profits realized from a strong-selling children's album.

2. *Limited returns.* There are very few returns with children music, basically because manufacturers provide adequate quality control for the pressings and the parents make the purchase. If the child does not like the recording, he or she simply ignores it.

3. *Longer shelf life.* While very few children's albums sell a lot of copies in a short amount of time like most pop hits, they do provide recordings that last year after year. Consequently, the retailer knows that in the long run this product will sell.

4. *Seldom obsolete.* Interest in a classic children's recording—such as *Peter Pan,* or *Snow White,* or a collection of classic favorites—lasts from generation to generation. Thus a recording will appeal to the next generation as well as it did to the previous generation—unlike pop hits that are usually outdated within several years.

5. *Airplay not required.* Since the labels do not have to compete with other musics for radio time, they avoid the costs and problems of promotion on the radio for their product.

Children's product is generally sold through the "celebrity concept." This means that a manufacturer will create a "character" and market a whole line of product—toys, games, books, clothing, and recordings—for consumers.

The way most children's characters achieve their celebrity status is through cartoon series, particularly on

Saturday morning television. Saturday morning has always been the prime time for children's television viewing. The reasons are simple and obvious: there is no school on Saturday mornings and parents generally like to sleep late so the children are allowed to watch whatever they wish on television as long as they don't wake their parents.

Manufacturers of children's products often produce television shows to popularize their characters and develop a market for their products, which they also merchandise. The Saturday morning slot on television provides very high profit margins for the TV networks and this leads to an ethical dilemma. First, there is not the prestige attached to Saturday morning TV like there is for prime time evening shows for network executives. Thus, the networks will generally pay less attention to the programming on Saturday morning. Too, the major advertisers—who are the source of revenue—are the ones bringing the new shows to the network. Many executives are reluctant to turn down a major advertiser who has a new show, especially if the show is high quality and solves a major problem for the network: what to program on Saturday morning.

The result is that consumers sometimes complain that the toy manufacturers are controlling the children who watch Saturday morning TV. Not only do they create characters and programs, they also bombard the children with a high ratio of advertising to programming and sometimes promote products that parents feel are not beneficial or advantageous to their children. They also promote a rampant materialism at any early age. Nevertheless, TV—and particularly Saturday morning TV—continues to provide the most effective means of reaching the nine-and-under audience.

Another way of reaching this audience is through movies directed at children. Walt Disney built an empire with this concept and his movies of *Cinderella, Pinocchio, Snow White* and numerous others have reached children for generations. These movies as well as movies developed from the TV characters have created another major market for children in the video generation: children's videos or "kid-vid." For parents who are busy, tired, or who want to provide the classic stories for their children, this is ideal. It has given rise to the concept of the "electronic babysitter" since children are content to watch these movies over and over.

The development of the cassette has been a major boon to the children's market for prerecorded music. The cassette is easier to handle than the records and small phonographs of the previous generations, less likely to scratch, skip, or develop the other problems that records are prone to, and is easily packaged with booklets and other print materials, which adds appeal.

The development of children's cassette recorders, first put on the market by Fisher-Price, also adds appeal to cassettes for children. These recorders are sturdy and give the child his or her own playback equipment, which does not have the problems presented by phonographs.

Major labels for children's product include Disneyland, which is the largest; Kid Stuff, which has characters such as Strawberry Shortcake, Raggedy Ann and Andy, Barbie and Pac Man; Peter Pan, the oldest which has characters like Casper the Friendly Ghost; and Sesame Street, which presents the Sesame Street characters seen on the *Sesame Street* television show every day on public television stations.

There are also crossovers with children's music. Movies such as *The Sound of Music, Mary Poppins, The Wizard of Oz, Annie,* and others have provided a market for albums to both the adult and children's market. There are also theme parks, such as Disneyland, Disneyworld, and others that present entertainment for children, as well as touring shows, such as Sesame Street, Smurfs, and others that reach the children's market. Periodicals such as *My Weekly Reader* among others provide access to this market as well.

In gospel music, the children's division of recording labels regularly returns high profits. This is because parents in this Christian culture want to raise their children with their faith and have found children's music an effective way of inculcating these values.

This brings us to the roles of children's music. This music is used to teach, educate, pass along classic stories and songs, as well as entertain children. The productions must be good—children are exposed to adult entertainment too and will not accept shoddy production—and must be entertaining as well as informative.

Children also like rock music on the radio and some rock acts have large followings of small children. These same children also watch Saturday morning TV, kid-vid, and listen to children's music. They do not want these entertainments to be any less "hip" or "contemporary," so manufacturers of children's products must always be aware that children are a sophisticated audience and cannot be reached by talking down to them or presenting product with inferior production or simple-minded themes.

The producers and manufacturers of children's music who are most successful have always been aware that they are dealing with timeless product that must also be contemporary. They must also be aware that it is the parents who purchase children's product, so the parents must be convinced it is worthwhile. But it is the children who generally ignite the initial demand and who, in the end, provide the lasting decision of whether the product really is worthy or not.

Ethnic Music

Ethnic music comes from, and primarily appeals to, a certain ethnic group. While there are a number of examples of ethnic music, two that play an especially significant part of independent labels in the recording industry are Latin music and Cajun music.

Latin music is important because of the growing number of Hispanics in America: in 1987 there were about 18.9 million Hispanics living in the United States (not counting 3.5 million in Puerto Rico). That figure is projected to climb to 25.2 million by 2000 and 59.6 million by 2080.

Over half of all Hispanic Americans live in Texas or California. The cities with greatest Hispanic populations are (in order) Los Angeles, New York, Miami, San Antonio, San Francisco, Chicago, Houston, McAllen/Brownsville (Texas), El Paso, and Albuquerque.

Latin America encompasses an area containing almost 30 countries with two European languages and embraces three cultures: European, African and Amerindian. Most of Latin America is Spanish-speaking, with Brazil speaking Portuguese. This Latin market consists of over 400 million people and the wholesale value of music sales in this market totals roughly $450 million annually, of which about 60 percent is derived from Spanish- or Portuguese-language recordings. Puerto Rico represents about 30 percent of Latin sales.

In the future, the South American and Caribbean Latin countries are expected to grow in population more rapidly than the United States, with a projected population of about 642 million by 2000—more than North America.

The common thread running throughout the Hispanic population in the United States is the Spanish language; in fact, a number of Hispanics living in the United States do not speak English. Another common thread is tremendous purchasing power.

However, there are divisions within the Hispanic culture, which is divided basically between Mexicans,

Cubans, and Puerto Ricans. Of the Hispanics in the United States, approximately 63 percent are Mexican, 12 percent are Puerto Rican, 11 percent come from Central and South America, about 5 percent from Cuba, and 9 percent are listed as "other."

It is projected that in the future Hispanics will become a larger minority than blacks in the United States. However, there seems to be a major difference between these two minorities in that Hispanics tend to assimilate into the mainstream culture more easily.

Musically, this is a diverse culture although there seem to be three basic categories of music: traditional folk Latino music, salsa, and pop music with Spanish lyrics. There is also samba, from Brazil, and bossa nova, another Brazilian music that combines jazz and samba. The tango comes from Argentina while salsa—the most pervasive influence in the United States—is a mixture of Spanish and African influences along with American jazz.

There are over 200 Spanish-language radio stations, two national Spanish TV networks with more than 240 affiliate channels, and numerous print publications in the United States. Additionally, some major newspapers (such as those in Miami and Los Angeles) have special sections printed in Spanish for the Hispanic populations, with other newspapers in key Hispanic markets also planning this strategy to reach the Hispanic consumer.

The Hispanic consumer is most readily reached through the Hispanic or Spanish-language media, which is growing in the United States. Their pop music is increasingly heard on mainstream rock/pop radio stations and receiving some coverage in mainline media. The product most appealing to this culture may be found in record stores located in areas with prominent Hispanic populations as well as independent stores in the Hispanic areas of cities with major Hispanic populations.

Cajun music is the music developed in the French-speaking area in Louisiana. It takes its name from Arcadia, the area in Canada from which these people emigrated before before settling in Louisiana. Cajun music is a lively, vibrant music, characterized by its link with the Cajun culture, a musical lineup that features the accordion prominently, French phrases and lyrics, and a unique swaying rhythm that captures the carefree attitudes of this music and culture.

Cajun is essentially a regional music, although it has a national appeal. Influential on a number of artists and popular music, the undiluted Cajun music is tied in with the Cajun culture—food, festivals and the like—and more limited in appeal than mainstream pop music.

People are attracted to Cajun music often because they are attracted to the culture. A major exposure has been festivals where food and culture as well as music are experienced. Radio airplay is extremely limited—again, college radio has proven to be the most fertile ground—and the most likely place to find a good, inclusive sampling of recordings for sales tends to be the megastores.

Often viewed as a folk or ethnic music, it is also sold through direct mail by catalogs, usually by firms who also sell folk and blues and other "roots" music recordings.

Folk Music

Folk music includes a wide variety of musics. There is the "authentic" folk music—either recorded in the field by true folk artists from the folk culture or contemporary artists recording such traditional material as "Barbara Allen," "St. James Infirmary" or other such roots material. There are also the singer/songwriters, who are increasingly called "folk" artists when they have limited production on their albums, as well as ethnic artists, such as those recording Cajun, polka, blues, or other kinds of ethnic music.

Actually, the term "folk music" has a number of connotations for professional folklorists. There is the notion that anything sung by the "folk," which may be broadly defined as the average, everyday person, is folk. Thus, songs on the radio that are picked up and sung regularly by the public become "folk songs." Others insist that folk music means the traditional roots music—Childe ballads, early folk songs passed down by oral tradition, and music from black and ethnic cultures. Still others say that "folk" means the music that comes out of a culture after being developed within that culture.

A good example of this latter example is rap music, which was the folk music for urban ghetto blacks before it caught the ear of pop artists and producers. The ways it spread were through the oral tradition—street corner performances—and through small, independent labels. Radio exposure is limited for folk music, although there are a number of programs on public radio that feature different varieties of folk music. Public television provides the major television exposure for this kind of music.

Folk music is heard most often in folk music festivals throughout the United States, Canada, and, indeed, the whole world. These festivals provide forums for singer/songwriters, traditional folk artists, and contemporary folk artists. Sometimes the festival features folk art, folk life, and other demonstrations of historical life in addition to the music.

There is some folk music stocked in record stores, particularly megastores and independent stores catering to this kind of music, but the primary marketing outlet is direct mail. This generally takes the form of catalogs listing folk recordings, sent regularly to mailing lists built up over decades. New names are added from someone writing in for information or from the festivals, which often feature booths and tables for folk artists and labels to sell their wares.

The "folk boom" of the 1960s created an awareness of folk music among many consumers who became rock buyers. Folk generally has a positive image with these buyers and many continue to buy folk recordings. This is generally a more affluent, up-scale audience, while other folk buyers may come from the college audience, who are generally more willing to experiment with their listening habits and more open to different kinds of music. College radio has provided a continuing forum for folk music and new buyers tend to come from the ranks of the college audience.

Blues

The first blues record (actually the first recording by a black artist, which was marketed to the black audience) was "Crazy Blues" by Mamie Smith in 1920. This was a "vaudeville blues" number and the success of this recording led to a number of other black female blues singers like Ma Rainey and Bessie Smith being recorded. This genre was dominated by women and the songs were generally written for the stage using the blues format. Beginning around 1926 recording executives began to do "field" recordings of rural blues singers. This rural or Delta blues was dominated by one singer—generally male—who played the guitar and sang. As blacks moved to the urban areas at the end of the nineteenth and beginning of the twentieth century, the blues changed and evolved by World War II to a band sound with electrical instruments that became known as rhythm and blues.

Two centers for the blues emerged: Memphis and Chicago. Memphis is generally characterized as a center for rural blues because so many blues singers came from the Mississippi Delta, south of Memphis. Chicago is recognized as the center for rhythm and blues, a music played by bands for dancing. However, the blues and rhythm and blues also developed in cities like Kansas City, Atlanta, Houston, Dallas, Los Angeles, St. Louis, Cincinnati, Detroit, New York and New Orleans.

The rural blues as an art form has almost disappeared from the black culture. Today, this form of blues—usually a singer accompanying himself on guitar—has been co-opted by white musicians who incorporate this style in their performances. Rhythm and blues has also been co-opted by white musicians, but there are also a large number of blacks playing this kind of music. It is generally hard driving, made for dancing in clubs, and characterized by a lineup that usually includes electric guitars, bass, drums, horns (usually saxophone), and sometimes harmonica.

Blues as a "roots" music consists of historical or catalog recordings of such greats as Leadbelly, Howlin' Wolf, Lightnin' Hopkins, Ma Rainey, Bessie Smith, Billie Holiday, Muddy Waters, and numerous other blues singers as well as current recordings by blues bands.

The megastore has been a good outlet for this music reaching mass consumers—and resulted in considerable sales—but the backbone of this music's sales has been the independent record store. These stores, independently owned and operated, have often served as a clearing house for information about concerts, groups forming, and new releases.

Since blues (particularly rhythm and blues) has long been acknowledged as a source for early rock 'n' roll as well as an influence on British musicians during their numerous invasions, record stores have usually been willing to stock some of these recordings. Radio airplay has been more difficult, limited to black radio and occasionally some public radio, although the college market—and college radio—has always been a good source of exposure for this music and these acts. Colleges have also been a rich source for blues concerts as well.

Marketing blues records has generally been heavily dependent upon groups touring and developing a following from numerous personal appearances. Direct mail has been a good way to reach core consumers, with catalogs containing new releases a way for consumers to find out about these recordings.

Bluegrass

Bluegrass and country music share much of the same heritage. But somewhere along the way there was a split, with country music heading toward a more mainstream audience with its "Nashville sound" and "pop crossover" appeal, while bluegrass stayed close to its traditional roots. Bluegrass features the traditional acoustic instruments of banjo, guitar, mandolin, dobro, and fiddle. The bass is often electrified now—basically because huge bass fiddles are so difficult to transport—and so are the vocals, but the image of bluegrass rests primarily on its appeal as a nonelectric kind of music.

There are numerous bluegrass festivals throughout the United States, particularly during the summers, and fans are known for playing the music as well as listening to it. Indeed, at most bluegrass festivals, there is often more music being played off the stage than there is on the stage. This is a community music—you are usually playing with an audience rather than at them.

Exposure on radio and television is limited, but there is a lively print media, with several magazines geared directly to the bluegrass devotee. Recordings are sold at festivals and through catalogs, developed from mailing lists whose length grows from names added from festival attendees.

There are a number of small, independent labels recording and marketing bluegrass. They keep production overheads low and sell 2,000 to 5,000 for an average release.

It is not mass market music, a fact that distinguishes it from country music, which is overtly commercial.

The bluegrass fans tend to be either college educated, exposed to this music during their college experience, or the traditional country fans, who like their music basic and unadorned. This second group is usually much less affluent, less educated, and more likely to see this music as part of their heritage.

There are some independent stores specializing in bluegrass, but the majority of sales for this music come from catalogs and other print media, such as the periodicals and direct mail sent to regular customers.

Spoken Word Recordings

Spoken word recordings are not music per se, but since they use the mediums of vinyl records, cassette tapes, and compact discs, this technology puts them in the sphere of the "recording industry."

Spoken word recordings may take the form of books, lectures, or talks on cassette, plays and other dramatic recordings, and speeches of notable people. For the record industry, the spoken word recordings marketed most often by major labels are comedy recordings.

The books-on-cassette concept has seen tremendous growth because of the number of cassette players in cars, the long drives to work by commuters, especially in large metropolitan areas, the popularity of portable technology like the Walkman, and the desire for consumers to have an alternative to radio when they are in their cars. Books on cassette are sold primarily through bookstores, which have accepted the recording technology into their stores when it is compatible with their book-buying public.

Comedy recordings have long been popular with the pop music audience, and a number of comics have had successful albums. The primary means of exposure for comedy artists is clubs, resorts, and television. Generally, it is television that has provided the key exposure for a successful comedy act. While movies also provide an important outlet for comedy acts, the primary means of exposure in pop music—radio—is extremely limited for most comedy acts.

The most successful comedy acts are generally viewed by the public as "recording artists" when they release an album and thus they are stocked and sold in regular retail outlets for recorded product.

Libraries and Educational Markets

Libraries, when they buy recordings, are most likely to buy spoken word recordings (books on cassette), dramatic recordings (plays), folk music (authentic), and classical recordings.

This market is rather small. There are approximately 200 libraries that regularly purchase recordings out of approximately 4,500 libraries in this country. The remaining number may purchase recordings occasionally.

The problems with marketing music to libraries are limited budgets; they are conditioned to buy books, they often do not know which particular albums should be purchased; and they are often not interested in stocking recordings. Basically, libraries have considered themselves repositories for books. The fact that they are becoming centers of information with computer terminals accessing data bases may be changing that a little, but it is doubtful change will occur to the point where all libraries regularly stock a large catalog of recordings.

There are three ways to market music to libraries: through their trade journals, through their annual meetings and conventions, and by direct mail.

9

Technology, Special Marketing, and Discography

When Thomas Edison developed the phonograph in 1877, the first recordings were made on tin cylinders. The development of the flat disc, by Emile Berliner in the late 1880s, led to the displacement of cylinders because the discs were easier to store and because the disc limited recording to professionals who recorded top talent and hence the recording companies could develop their own market.

The first configuration to dominate the music industry was the 78 rpm record, made of shellac. This configuration had a remarkably long career—for over 40 years it was the only way prerecorded music was sold. That changed in 1948 when CBS presented the first long playing album (LP). This was followed by the introduction of the 45 rpm single by RCA in 1950. After some initial jostling in the marketplace to determine whether the 33 or 45 rpm would dominate, it was finally settled that the 33 rpm would be the format for albums while the 45 rpm would be the format for singles. These two configurations—the 45 and 33 rpm vinyl records—dominated the industry for over 20 years and made the marketing decision about which configuration to place in the market automatic because there was no competing configuration for consumers. That is no longer the case.

Recording tape was developed by the Germans during World War II. After the War, the Allies seized some of the tape equipment and studied it, adapted it to use in studios, and thus revolutionized the recording process. (Previously, recordings had been made direct to disc.) The cassette tape format was developed by the Dutch firm Philips, in 1964. Within a few years, it was increasingly finding acceptance with music lovers, even though it was originally developed as a business machine. However, the record companies first ignored the format, developing eight-track tapes instead.

Actually, the record companies tended to look down on both tape formats—cassette and eight-track—in the 1960s and early 1970s, viewing the configuration as inferior to the vinyl 33s and 45s. But consumers accepted them readily as the tape transformed listening habits radically by making music portable. Previous to this, if you wanted to listen to an album, you had to sit down in front of a console. The only "portable" music was the small phonographs teenagers carried to parties with their 45s. But here again, the machine had to be plugged in and the dancers had to be careful lest the records skip.

With tapes, people could listen to their favorite albums in their cars, on the beach, or wherever else they wanted to go. And the tapes consumers preferred were eight-tracks. The sound quality was better than cassettes at the time and they were easy to handle. The major problem was a big gap where the tape switched tracks. This was not an insurmountable problem—a little planning from the record companies would have ensured that no gaps would fall in the middle of a song. However, the record companies simply took the same tape made for the vinyl album and made an eight-track tape, which meant that big gaps often fell right in the middle of a song. The companies created more ill will for themselves in their marketing. Often they would not release an album on tape or, if they did, it would come several weeks—or even months—after the vinyl album and would be priced higher, usually by one or two dollars. The tape was really an afterthought, thrown into the marketplace with near disdain.

Consumers responded by home-taping albums, and tape pirates had a field day, selling tapes they had dubbed from albums without paying any royalties to artists or record companies. The companies were upset and sought to clamp down on the pirates, which they eventually did, but many still didn't quite get the message that they should pay more attention to the tape configuration. The problem of tape vs. vinyl was further compounded by retailers who did not like tape for several reasons. First, it was too easy to steal, so theft was a major problem. They responded by locking the tapes inside glass cases, putting them out of reach of consumers, and other ways that made even honest consumers feel like criminals. Too, the record stores were built for records, with the bins the size of albums, and floor layout for vinyl albums. But most important, the attitude was that they were *record* stores. It was a tradition hard to break.

Several things happened to change all of this. First, Ford signed a deal with Motorola, in 1967, to put cassette tape players in cars as an incentive for buyers. Ford had realized the appeal of a tape player in a car and so had Motorola; they made the decision to go with cassettes instead of eight-tracks. (This came as a result of the development of the noise reduction system for cassettes by physicist Ray Dolby.) Next, retailers became aware that their consumers wanted more than just records in record stores. They wanted things like record cleaners, cartridges, and posters and tapes—both blank and prerecorded. So retailers began stocking all of this. The record companies, miffed that pirates had siphoned off so much profit with back-room bootlegging, began taking a good hard look at tape and decided to develop cassettes and de-emphasize the eight-track format. This was in direct response to the Ford/Motorola deal.

But the record companies still did not respect the consumers enough to manufacture top-quality tapes, and the result was that consumers began buying a significant number of blank tapes, marketed aggressively by blank tape companies who saw the potential, and home taping became a major problem. Finally, by the end of the 1970s and beginning of the 1980s, the record companies realized that consumers demanded tapes, that they needed to be top quality, and that marketing plans should consider this market and go after it more aggressively. By 1982, cassettes were selling almost as well as vinyl albums; by 1983, they were about equal, and after that time the cassette configuration consistently outsold the vinyl LP.

The cassette revolutionized the music industry because it made music portable. This changed how—and where—we listen to music and affected music in radical ways. For instance, in the 1980s, music began to be viewed as an accompaniment to jogging, walking, driving, aerobics, and other activities. The notion of sitting down in front of a home stereo system to listen to an album all the way through has not disappeared, but it is now only one way to listen to music, a way that fewer people engage in. Many would rather listen to music on the move.

The cassette made music even more pervasive. A walk in the country or in the woods is now often accompanied by music instead of silence and even farmers on tractors in the middle of a huge field can listen to their favorite album. It also made international marketing much easier because the cassette format could be marketed in places without the access to electricity developed countries have long enjoyed, as well as in countries with extreme heat or cold, and in countries with limited living and storage spaces. It also enabled people in numerous countries to enter the tape-duplicating and music distribution business without the huge overhead of a pressing plant necessary for vinyl albums. The success of the cassette has also made a subtle change in our language: an "album" is not assumed to be a vinyl LP anymore but rather any configuration with a collection of songs.

The vinyl album was challenged mightily by the cassette tape configuration in the 1980s, but the compact disc format may have been the deciding factor in the near total demise of vinyl albums. The CD configuration was introduced at the end of 1983 and within two years had achieved a significant portion of the recorded music market. By 1988, retailers noted that the cassette was the major selling configuration, followed by CDs, with vinyl LPs a distant third, accounting for only about 10 percent of the market.

For record companies marketing recorded product, this presents a major problem. Since no one configuration dominates the music industry like the vinyl LP used to, which configuration should be manufactured for an act? In spite of the demise of the vinyl LP, companies cannot ignore the LP market. For one thing, there are too many turntables and too many LPs out in the market. Next is the problem of consumer confusion and, worse, the prospect of incurring the ire and wrath of consumers. This happened before when record companies decided to switch from the eight-track format in favor of cassettes. To do this, they dumped an enormous number of eight-tracks on the market at greatly reduced prices. Eight-track machines were also sold at cut-rate prices in order to liquidate stocks. The result was that numerous consumers, seeing that the eight-track was a better buy than cassettes—for which tapes and machines cost more—bought eight-tracks in large numbers. A few years later they realized they could no longer find their favorite artists on eight-track and that they had been "had" by these companies. There are still a lot of eight-tracks out in consumers homes, garages, and cars, and some consumers have never forgiven the record companies for what they did.

The rest have learned to be very wary of any new configurations. These people were reluctant to switch to compact discs and some still wonder if this configuration, too, will soon be part of the past.

The cassette configuration also creates a dilemma for recording companies. There is no one format for cassettes—there are chromium dioxide cassettes, metal tape, and other high-quality formats. And there is also the microcassette, whose smaller size is even more appealing for those who carry their music with them, although it has failed to catch on in the American market like it has with the Japanese.

Before cassette tapes, the alternative to LPs was the reel-to-reel tape. This configuration was aimed at audiophiles and was the highest quality analog format ever marketed. However, it never caught on as well as cassettes (or eight-tracks) because it was too inconvenient for consumers, who had to thread it on large cumbersome machines, and because the price was much higher than that for LPs. Too, the companies backed off this configuration during the tape bootleggers' heyday in the late 60s and early 70s because bootleggers could make a much better dub from a reel-to-reel tape.

The end result is that marketing departments must now confront technology when they draw up their marketing plan. It is obvious that a major act will have product in a wide variety of configurations: cassette, high-quality cassette, video, and compact disc. The question comes with new acts: How much of each configuration should be put in the market for consumers?

These are all questions that add to the day-to-day decision-making for record releases. And they add costs and create problems with planning. In the past, if an act's vinyl LPs did not sell, that was bad; but if an act has product out in CD, cassette, high-quality cassette, video, and vinyl, and if none of these sell, it can be disastrous. Too, there are scheduling problems. The vinyl albums would come out of one plant and so one phone call could check on progress. But there are different manufacturing facilities for CDs, cassettes, and videos—some not even in this country. All of this must be coordinated, which becomes a major job in itself. Especially when the graphics for each of these configurations is different and perhaps comes from different locations as well. The person doing marketing must therefore confront technology every day. If the plans are wrong, this can cost the company huge amounts of money as well as the problem of overstocked product; on the other hand, consumers wanting to buy a particular configuration may be unable to obtain it.

There is also the problem of introducing new technology into the marketplace. The introduction of CDs, in 1983, into the market resulted in huge profits for recording labels; first, they had to charge higher prices because of the higher manufacturing costs, but as manufacturing costs decreased, recording labels kept their prices high because consumers had become accustomed to the higher prices. This resulted in a huge windfall of profits for the labels. Too, consumers did not just buy current product: they replaced old LPs with compact discs, and the sale of these catalog albums, along with the development of boxed sets (creatively packaged particular kinds of music or an artist's entire career output), further added to profits

By the end of 1983, when the CD was introduced, consumers were purchasing current LPs but no catalog items in significant numbers. The idea that a new technology will spur new sales as consumers buy catalog product in the new technology, like they did with CDs, is a powerful lure for music industry marketers. Also, there are two major recording labels—Sony and Polygram that are owned by firms who make hardware. These firms know that if they release a new technology into the market they also have a great deal of material or software to put on it, so they have an edge in introducing new technology.

Technology is ahead of the consumer market because there are new developments constantly. But consumers do not have the means to constantly buy new technology and do not want to purchase new technology incompatible with their existing home systems. It was a major shift from vinyl LPs to CDs because consumers had to purchase new hardware *and* software. The question arises: Would consumers do it again? For the music industry the question has an added dimension: Would consumers do it again and again and again? If new technology provides a surge in new profits, the temptation is to saturate the market with new technology and new configurations. But most consumers are reluctant to continually invest in new technology and new configurations; most would simply rather stick with technology they are satisfied with and purchase new software.

This puts the recording industry at an interesting crossroads: There will be diminished profits if and when consumers reduce their spending on catalog purchases, but there may be a loss of consumer confidence and also diminished profits if a new technology is put into the market but not accepted by buyers. This question is especially difficult for those companies who also market hardware.

In many ways the 1980s was a decade of technology and the story of marketing music in the 80s is the story of changes and shifts in technology. In addition to the development of the compact disc and digital technology, there was also the development of music on cable TV, led by the introduction of MTV in 1981, and the development of the video industry throughout the 1980s. At the beginning of the 1980s, few people had video cassette recorders (VCRs) and there were few video rental stores; the habits of TV watchers did not generally include video rentals or taping TV shows. For the music industry, music videos were not a significant part of the marketing of an act. However, by the end of the 1980s the video industry was a major part of American culture and music videos were a major format for prerecorded music. This shift in technology changed the look of music marketing and added a dimension to music in the market.

Before the 1980s the recording industry was dominated by the vinyl record heard on radio and purchased at mall stores; by the end of the 1980s the recording industry was dominated by the compact disc heard on radio and seen on music videos and purchased primarily at mass merchandisers or in free-standing stores. But though there were huge changes in technology and trends in retailing, the basic principles of getting music in the market remained basically the same as they had been for years.

Special Marketing

Special marketing may be defined as selling prerecorded music anywhere outside the mainstream outlets. The mainstream outlets are racks in mass merchandisers and record stores; thus special marketing encompasses sales on TV, through record clubs, direct mail, or in outlets such as grocery stores, clothing stores, convenience markets, and at conventions. However, most in the music industry tend to refer to special marketing as TV sales.

There are three reasons why special marketing has grown during the past decade: technology, advertising, and demographics.

It is hard to believe that television and telephones are considered "high tech" because they have been part of our homes for so long. Yet they are high tech and the developments in these two areas have made it possible for albums to be sold directly to consumers in their homes. The major reasons for the success of TV marketing are credit cards, toll free numbers, and overnight delivery. These factors have made TV shopping part of impulse buying and displaced the old method of TV shopping where the consumer had to write and request a product advertised, wait six to eight weeks for a C.O.D. delivery, then try to remember why they wanted the product two months previously. For companies that marketed this way, there was a major problem because if a customer refused a C.O.D. order, then the sender had to pay all the costs. Thus for marketers as well as consumers, TV shopping had too many drawbacks to be either satisfying or profitable.

Television has made a number of changes and advances in recent years. The development of TV in a variety of formats (large-screen, portables, Watchmans, stereo) and the fine-tuning of color TV with an accompanying drop in prices for color TV has led to the demise of the black-and-white sets as well as the corresponding access to high quality TV in almost every home in the United States. Currently, about 98 percent of American homes have television and many have more than one set. It is also significant to note that of the 2 percent of households that do not have a TV, the major reason is that the householders have chosen not to have television, not that they can't afford television or are unable to have it (because of lack of electricity or the unavailability of sets). In addition to the development of the picture, television manufacturers also have developed better sound, resulting in stereo TV.

Perhaps the biggest breakthrough in television has been the creation and acceptance of numerous cable and local channels with the resulting reduction of the power and control of the networks. Consumers now have a wide choice in their TV viewing and, with television available 24 hours a day seven days a week there is an endless demand for programming. Currently, the TV set may be used to watch rented movies, play video games, as a screen for home computers, to watch home videos made with homeowner video cameras and to tape scheduled programming to watch at a later time (time-shifting).

With so many cable and local channels the possibilities have opened up to advertise in a particular market or region at a reasonably low rate. Too, the number of stations competing for the advertiser's dollar has created business situations in which the station will assume part of the risk. This has all benefited advertisers of prerecorded product.

In some cases, the TV packager may approach a local market, try a product and, if it does well, move on to other markets or do a national campaign. Or, the product may be dropped. A deal may also be worked out where the packager will get free air time on a station in exchange for a percentage of the income received from a package. This allows the advertiser to minimize their risk while the station has the chance to make a good amount of money if the ad is successful.

The way people order these TV packages is by dialing an 800 (toll free) number and reading their credit card number over the phone. This brings up several advances in telecommunications. First, telephones can do much more than they used to and, in effect, link us to the entire world as well as to a world of services and products. The development of the 800 number system allows consumers to order a product without having to pay for the call—an inducement business is eager to accept. Too, the spread of credit cards throughout all income levels in America—instead of just being available to those with high incomes—has allowed lower- and middle-income households to shop and buy more merchandise. The credit card has also eliminated several of the most costly problems in television marketing—bad checks and C.O.D. orders.

Advertisers now have many more outlets on television than they had in the past at much better rates than those from the network. Too, advertisers don't just want to reach people—they want a specific segment of the population and TV has increasingly been able to target their viewers—at least target them more than in the past.

Television is a major source of entertainment for those over 25. As the population gets older, they are more likely to stay home and watch television. The 25-to-55-year-olds have traditionally bought albums and are likely to continue to do so in stores. The younger buyers—10 to 25—are less likely to be reached via a TV package; they also prefer the social interaction of a store.

Direct Mail

A number of people in this country do not shop regularly in stores. These people prefer to shop by catalog for a variety of reasons: their careers keep them too busy to shop, they do not like shopping, the times when it is most convenient for them to shop the stores are closed, or they prefer looking through catalogs at leisure instead of fighting traffic and other people to try and find what they want. Direct mail has become a major way for many people to shop.

In the record industry there is another reason: what people want may not be available in their local stores. Since retailers have often been unable to stock as much product as the consumers have demanded, particularly in catalog product, consumers have had to get those albums from direct mail. The record clubs have helped here, providing a large selection and accounting for about 10-15 percent of total record sales. They have increasingly sought to target their consumers with classical or other specialty offerings.

Too, classical music, jazz, bluegrass, folk, and certain other types of music are not generally stocked in quantity in an "average" record store. So the connoisseurs of these kinds of music have had to get their albums from direct mail. The recording companies for this music have long realized this and supplied catalogs to their consumers, enabling them to order a wide selection from the company's catalog.

Market Research

First, a definition of market research: It is *asking questions and analyzing the answers about a company, product or market,* or *the study of the demands or needs of consumers in relation to particular goods or services.*

In conducting market research, the researcher must be aware of primary and secondary data resources. Primary data come from new information collected from people and organizations. Secondary data sources are repositories of data originally collected for some other purpose. For example, studying a particular market, secondary data might include the census for the population as well as other facts like average income, source of employment, and average age. Primary data would be information about the buying habits of people for a particular kind of music.

There are six major data collection methods:

1. *Experiment.* Generally linked to science and not usually used for research into the music industry.

2. *Survey.* This is an important data collection method for most music industry research. It involves drawing up questionnaires and conducting campaigns to collect data.

3. *Observation.* This is important because when dealing with consumer habits in record stores, perhaps the layout of the store is important, or store traffic, or other factors that can be determined simply by watching.

4. *Simulation.* Usually used with focus groups—small gatherings of people led by a group leader—and an important source for information on a number of issues and

questions in the music industry. For example, radio consultants often play recordings to ascertain a listener's reaction.

5. *Qualitative techniques.* These are psychological motivations, generally called psychographics, which come from asking why people do what they do.

6. *Electronic.* This involves computers downloading sales and airplay data and has become the *major* market research methodology for data collection in the music industry, especially since the development of bar codes and bar code scanners at retail.

For a number of years, the music industry ran on intuition, "gut reaction" they called it, in making most major decisions. Their reasoning was that no one could "predict" a hit or a star so you should rely on someone with the right "ears" to pick hits. Further, since the public was fickle, it was hopeless to do research because nothing could accurately predict the taste of the public. Compounding this philosophy is the fact that music is emotional and reaches people on an emotional level; thus logic and intellect—which can be measured—are irrelevant, and decisions must be made emotionally.

This view changed dramatically in 1977 when Warner Brothers released the first in-depth research in the music industry. Several old fallacies were shot: the notion that "the kids buy all the records" was replaced by the statistics that the 10 to 22 demographic purchased about 40 percent of recordings, but the 25 to 44 demographic also purchased about 40 percent. Other interesting facts were uncovered: that 50 percent of all purchases of recordings in December were as gifts, and that consumers could be categorized into continuous, non-continuous, and non-buyers of music.

This market research by Warner Brothers came at a time when American business in general was depending more and more on market research. Although at times it seems that the tail is wagging the dog with market research—managers often believe that more facts will make the decision for them and totally ignore intuitive or "gut level" responses to problems—the fact is that market research has become an integral part of decision making.

Perhaps the most significant bit of market research has come from the data collection methods of *Billboard*, with the information gathered on radio airplay, and SoundScan, which has used bar code technology to collect accurate data on the number of albums sold. Recording industry executives can look at computer printouts and see quickly where an album is selling well and send more product into that market; this information allows them to react to the market more quickly and effectively. This information also shows what *kind* of music is being accepted best by consumers and where the market is soft for product.

The most difficult questions to answer are those connected with the creative process, those which would help an executive determine new musical trends, what consumers look for in a recording or artist, why people like a particular song or artist, and how people decide when to purchase a product. Focus groups, which are small groups who gather and give verbal feedback to someone who directs the group, have provided some insight into these questions and allowed labels to "test" an artist or album before it is released.

Discography

Discography is the cataloging of information about recordings. It is important because it gives an accurate, detailed account of recordings for researchers and historians. For the record company executive it is important because it informs him or her what is in the record company's inventory.

Most music business executives know only current product—perhaps an album or two back—because their jobs entail working current releases. Once a single is off the charts, or an album no longer current, active, and selling, the executive will drop this project and go on to another current one. While this is the nature of the music business executive's job, and it is essential that the company consistently create viable new commercial product, there are some drawbacks. Most of the major labels have been in business a long time—almost a century in some cases—and the executive who does not have a working knowledge of this extensive catalog is at a decided disadvantage when making decisions about re-releases of older product, the leasing of certain older product, and the potential purchase or sale of recordings in the vault.

An example: One major label paid over $1 million for a particular company's catalog, thinking they were buying a number of valuable unreleased cuts. However, once the material was purchased, it was discovered that a number of the "unreleased" cuts were merely other "takes." Before multitrack recordings became commonplace, it was not unusual for an artist to record several "takes" of a song—essentially, the same arrangement and production several times. These would be used as backups and, in some cases, were available for pressings if it was necessary to have several press runs to fill orders. These takes did not differ substantially from what the public already knew and thus were not really "valuable." Too, a number of the cuts had been released in the international market and been purchased by stores as imports—thus the notion that they had never been released domestically was misleading. A good working knowledge of discography—and the use of a discographer—could have solved these problems.

There are other instances where executives have made major mistakes because they simply did not know what was in their company's inventory, by leasing cuts or albums that should not have been released, or by failing to understand the market for a particular artist or song or album when they were re-packaging vintage items.

Too, many decisions regarding whether an established artist should be signed or not or whether an "oldie" should be re-recorded and released are based on discographical information. For example, before signing an established act who has not had a hit in several years, the label may want to know how many albums are currently on the market, when the last hit recording was, how well it did on the charts and how many hit singles and albums the act has had. For a song, the number of times it has been released as a single, the last time it was on the charts, how well it did on the charts, and who else has released it as a single are all important marketing considerations.

Several important sources give information vital to marketing executives. The *Phonologue* is a huge book that lists all the recordings currently on the market. (You may also track down the albums available in the market in *Schwann*'s, which is available in most record stores.) Other excellent source books are Joel Whitburn's books on *Billboard*'s charts. Whitburn has a number of books out based on a number of charts—country, R & B, pop, singles and albums—and here you can find every song, artist, and album that has appeared on a *Billboard* chart. These sources are invaluable when tracking the history of an artist or song. Several labels—including Atlantic and RCA—have books of discography on their early releases and some top acts, such as the Beatles, Elvis Presley, and Bob Dylan, also have books devoted to their discographies.

There are several terms important to know regarding discography. The *control number* is the number assigned to each recording by the label. If several different recordings are made during a particular session, there will be a different control number assigned to each cut. The *commercial release number* is the number consumers see on an album jacket or record/tape label. An album will have one commercial release number though there are ten different recordings on the label. The *catalog number* is the number assigned to a recording by the company for use in ordering from stores and other customers. *Reissue* is the term used for any recording appearing any time other than the original release. *Repackaging* is essentially the same recording but a different album cover or configuration.

Other terms to be cognizant of: *Alternative take*: used in the past before overdubbing. Means essentially the same song recorded the same way (as to production and arrangement) and available for commercial use. *Overdubbing:* the adding on of instruments and voices after the original recording session. Today a number of recordings are made over a long time period, involving several studios, cities, and musicians who may not have been in the studio at the same time as other musicians or the artists. This idea of overdubbing and multitracking makes discography difficult today because there is no one set recording date when everything happens, as in the early days of recording.

Other valuable sources for discography are the list of "gold" and "platinum" albums released by the Recording Industry Association of America (RIAA); the list of Grammy winners from the National Association of Record Merchandisers (NARM); and books like *Million Sellers,* which lists million-selling songs since 1904.

There are eight basic types of discography: numerical, session or studio listings, artist, musical genre, song, filmusicography or videography, bio-discography, and composer discography.

Numerical discography is the simplest. It consists of listing, in order of number, releases from a label or label series. The number used is either the release number or the catalog number. This is most useful when doing a discography of a particular label or series on a label.

The *session or studio listings* discography is a list of recordings done at a particular studio or on particular sessions in a particular time period. This type of discography is not particularly applicable in contemporary music—so many studios are used for a recording and the use of overdubbing extends a session over periods of times and several musicians—but is useful when looking at a time when recordings were made by a particular group of sidemen or at a particular place. Here can be examined the influence of Houston or Dallas or Sun's Studio in Memphis or Bradley's Barn in Nashville on the music of the time.

An *artist discography* is the most common type. Here, all the recordings of a particular artist are listed in chronological order. There are two subgenres here: the complete discography and the representative type. There are also differences on what is recorded on this discography: musicians, songwriters, publishing companies, dates of recording, dates of release, highest position on the charts, and studio where the song(s) were recorded may all be either added or deleted in discographies.

The *musical genre discography* involves picking a particular type of music—Cajun, string quartets, honky-tonk, for example—and doing a discography using the releases that are appropriate to this music. The major problem is being very specific on the genre so that it does not get out of hand. For example, you would not want to do a musical genre discography on "rock" or "pop" music.

A *song discography* traces a particular song—particularly one that has been recorded a great deal like "Yesterday" or "Gentle on My Mind"—through all its recordings.

A *filmusicography* or *videography* is a discography dealing with musical performances preserved in any sort of film or video form. These may include movies, TV shows, or videos.

The *bio-discography* is similar to the artist discography except that other commentary is added between listings. This information may include biographical information about what the artist was doing at the time of these particular recordings, relevant stories about songs or personnel on the recordings, or the effect this particular song/session had on the artist's career.

The *composer discography* lists the compositions written by a particular songwriter.

In summary, there are good practical reasons why a record company executive should know about discographical information. Some of the practical applications of discographical information are as follow: (1) for a company's reissues and repackages; (2) for leasing arrangements (such as for TV packages, direct mail repackaging and international releases); (3) song research—finding out who has previously recorded a song and its success on the charts; (4) repackaging older recordings by an artist who has suddenly achieved popularity; (5) for uses in film and advertising (often requiring leasing and licensing arrangements); (6) for inventory control and asset evaluation; and (7) for contract evaluation as well as artist histories and publicity releases.

Conclusion

The music industry is a combination of music, technology, and business. It is a major influence on popular culture and is, in turn, heavily influenced by popular culture. To understand the music industry it is necessary to study the context in which it exists; that context involves the marketing of music to consumers. It is not possible to fully understand the music of popular culture—popular music in its variety of forms—without understanding the commercial market that makes culture popular through its appeal to the mass audience.

To look at the music industry as a consumer is to see only a small portion—the end product, as it were—of an artist in concert, in the media, or in a configuration to purchase. At this point, the artist and consumer connect through music and this connection can be powerful; listeners are often deeply touched by an artist, a song, or just music. This is an emotional connection and is the very essence of music. Without this emotional connection, the music business is irrelevant.

To look at the music industry as an artist is to look at a career, a calling, and perhaps a vision. It is a way to make a living at the same time it is an expression of the heart, soul, and mind. But to look at the industry from the perspective of an artist just by looking at the music itself is to miss key elements of getting the music from the artist to the audience. Every successful artist is part of the star-making machine, and every successful artist must look at this field as more than just music—it is a business as well.

The music industry has changed a great deal since Edison invented the phonograph in 1877. The technology has gone from cylinders to discs, from primitive gramophones to sophisticated home stereo systems, from recording on tinfoil to recording on digital tape. The leap in technology over a period of about a hundred years is almost too overwhelming to imagine, yet we take for granted that even greater leaps in technology will occur in the future.

The business structure has changed as well. The development of the first two major recording labels, Victor and Columbia, occurred at the beginning of the twentieth century. A system of recording and manufacturing records was developed, and there were developments in other technologies (radio and television), which changed the business structure as the recording industry developed ways to market and sell recordings. In every step of the way it was the profit motive that kept business people moving forward; because the recording industry held the potential for large profits, business people entered it. And when large profits were made, others joined while marketing strategies were continually developed and refined to expand the market and sell more recordings.

The vehicle was the music, of course. Because it was profitable to sell music, people sold it; because people bought music—and wanted it in their lives—it became influential. So a cycle of demand was created: business demanded profits, which were supplied by consumers who demanded recorded music, which demanded artists to record this music, which demanded technology to capture this music. This circle became a giant wheel, rolling through history.

In this book we have looked at the music industry from the business perspective because that is the key to understanding how the music gets from the artist to the consumer. We are all consumers and what we consume most becomes popular culture. But we are also in the business of earning a living and this business of earning a living creates the incomes to purchase access to this music. The artists are also in the business of earning a living, and those who work in the music business are in the business of providing entertainment to be enjoyed in our homes. These are the middlemen of popular culture, and this book is a look at these middlemen. In looking at popular music, it is easy to study the source—the artists who give us this music—and it is easy to study the consumer because we are all consumers. But the middlemen are often overlooked. This book is an attempt to examine the middlemen of popular music in order to help understand the music itself.

Appendix

Income and Costs of a Recording Label

The book discusses the way a recording label spends money and how it makes money; here is a more detailed look at the costs and income for a recording label.

To calculate the P & P (pressing and printing), otherwise known as "manufacturing" cost of an album, simply multiply the number pressed by the cost of each. For example, if there are 10,000 CDs pressed, and they cost $1.30 each to press, then it is 10,000 x $1.30 = $13,000.

Since several different configurations are generally pressed, this formula applies to each. For example, if there are 10,000 cassettes pressed at $1.25 each and 20,000 CDs pressed at $1.30 each, then the calculation is:

10,000 x $1.25 = $12,500
20,000 x $1.30 = $26,000
$12,500 + $26,000 = $38,500

The next step in figuring up the cost for an album involves "recoupables," or those charges incurred by the label which are "charged back," and thus ultimately paid for, by the artist through royalties earned from sales. For example, the production costs of the album—the amount paid for studios, a producer, musicians—are all held against artist royalties until these costs are paid back to the label. So are other costs such as advances to the artist for living expenses, tour support, advertising and marketing campaigns, and other promotional expenses. Although each artist's contract is different, in most cases anything beyond the normal promotional and marketing efforts—like putting together a basic bio and picture for a press kit and phone calls by promotion people to radio stations—is a potential charge back to the artist.

Major artists often negotiate for the label to pay a significant amount of marketing costs without being charged back for them. This label commitment may include advertisements in major publications, some POP (point-of-purchase) material, and perhaps even financial support for a "talk tour" where the artist goes to radio stations, retail and distribution accounts and selected media in a number of cities to meet and greet those involved with marketing the album as well as do interviews. But in most cases, all expenses the label picks up will ultimately be charged against the artist.

Before an album is available for sale in the marketplace, a number of costs have been paid for by the recording label. For example, by the time an album has reached the store and *before* the first sale is made, the label has had to pay manufacturing costs, production costs and other recoupables, and some basic marketing costs, such as putting together press kits. The label attempts to offset these up-front expenses by negotiating discounts in their payments—in effect, paying artist royalties for only a portion of the albums sold.

The two most "popular" discounts are "breakage" and "packaging." The "breakage" discount is usually 10 percent of the total sold and dates back to the time when records were made of shellac and thus easily breakable. Since it was assumed that about 10 percent of all records shipped would break in transit, the label began a "breakage allowance" in order to pay for only 90 percent of records sold so they could recover their losses. Even though shellac was replaced by vinyl, which was in turn replaced by cassette tapes and compact discs, this "breakage allowance" has remained and labels routinely begin negotiations with this in the artist's contract.

The other discount labels seek is "packaging," which has its roots in the elaborate packages that artists put together in the 1960s. Some of these packages were extensive—foldouts and overlays—and did cost extra. Later, the CD jewel box became an additional expense. This "packaging" discount is also usually 10 percent.

If a label is able to negotiate both the breakage and packaging discount, then they receive a 20 percent discount from product sold; in other words, they only have to pay artist royalties on 80 percent of the albums sold to consumers.

Once an album is in stores, available for consumers, a recording label can begin receiving income. It is *only* through the sale of recordings—not radio airplay, TV airplay, or artist tours—that a label receives any income.

In order to compute gross income for the label, simply multiply the wholesale cost of the album by the number sold. For example, if the label shipped 50,000 CDs at a wholesale cost of $8.50 per CD, then the gross income would be:

$$50{,}000 \times \$8.50 = \$425{,}000$$

Since albums are regularly sold in several different configurations—CDs, cassettes, and videos are the most prevelant—the wholesale cost of each, multiplied by the number shipped, is computed, then these totals are added together for gross income. For example, if a label shipped 80,000 CDs at $8.50 each and 20,000 cassettes at $6.50 each, the computation would go as follows:

$$80{,}000 \times \$8.50 = \$680{,}000$$
$$20{,}000 \times \$6.50 = \$130{,}000$$
$$\$680{,}000 + \$130{,}000 = \$810{,}000$$

In order to compute a label's net income, several costs must be subtracted from this gross. First, there is the cost of manufacturing. Assuming the album sold 100,000 copies, 80,000 in CDs and 20,000 in cassettes, and the CDs cost $1.25 each to manufacture and the cassettes cost $1.05 each, this calculation would be performed:

80,000 x $1.25 = $100,000
20,000 x $1.05 = $21,000
$100,000 + $21,000 = $121,000 in manufacturing costs

This calculation of manufacturing costs does not include the promotional copies of recordings sent to radio stations and other media to promote the artist's career. These are part of the label's normal costs of doing business and are not recoupable from the artist's earnings. If there were 4,000 CDs and 1,000 cassettes sent out for promotional purposes, then the additional costs would be:

4,000 x $1.25 = $5,000
1,000 x $1.05 = $1,050
$5,000 + $1,050 + $121,000 = $127,050 in manufacturing costs

To determine the label's cost adjusted for manufacturing, subtract the manufacturing costs from the gross amount received:

$810,000 - $127,050 = $682,950

A label must pay music publishers a statutory rate for use of songs on albums sold. Currently, that rate is $.066 cents per song on each album. So, if an album contains 10 songs, then the label is obligated to pay $.66 to publishers for each album sold.

This money is usually collected by the Harry Fox Agency, which charges a 3.5 percent collection fee and sends the rest to the publisher. The publisher then pays the writer half and keeps half of these "mechanicals," a term derived from fees assessed piano rolls when the 1909 Copyright Act was enacted. It does not matter what the configuration or wholesale price is, the statutory rate is set by law for labels to pay. This rate was first established by the 1978 Copyright Law and has provisions for the rate to increase through the years.

In the album discussed, if the label sold 100,000 albums, and then had to pay $.66 for each album, the label must pay the publishers $66,000 from these sales. Thus, we have another figure to subtract in order to determine gross income:

$682,950 - $66,000 = $616,950

The labels generally seek a "controlled composition" clause in contracts whereby they will pay 75 percent of the statutory rate. Often, this is used with artists who write their own material—the singer/songwriter—with the rationale that the 25 percent the label does not pay the songwriter in mechanicals will be invested in his/her career via marketing. However, a label often seeks the "controlled composition" clause for an entire album and puts the burden on the artist (and his/her manager) to negotiate these lesser fees with publishers.

If the controlled composition clause was enacted on this album of 10 songs, then the label would pay 75 percent of $.66, or $.495 cents for each album sold. This would lower costs dramatically:

100,000 x $.495 = $49,500

Although the statutory rate is set at $.066 per song on an album, a label will sometimes give the artist a budget; for example, they might say they will pay $.495 for each album sold no matter how many songs are on the album. It will then be up to the artist to negotiate with publishers for a smaller amount or else come up with the money out of his/her own pocket. This generally has the effect of lowering the number of songs on an album, which is a major reason an American album generally has 10 songs on it, despite the fact that CDs can hold more music.

Artist royalties may be based on either wholesale price or suggested retail price. The "suggested retail price" of an album is what the label suggests—the retailers are not bound to sell the album for that amount. And, in fact, few retailers sell for "suggested retail" because the market is so competitive.

If an artist's royalty is 15 percent of wholesale price and the wholesale price is $8.75 for a CD, then the artist receives:

$$\$8.75 \times .15 = \$1.3125$$

This means that for each album sold, the artist receives $1.3125 in royalties. However, if the label receives its 20 percent discount for breakage and packaging, the artist would only receive 80 percent of that or:

$$\$1.3125 \times .80 = \$1.05 \text{ per album}$$

Recording labels usually claim they only break even on 20 percent of all albums released—and that 80 percent of all their product loses money. However, the break-even is determined from the *artist's* break-even point, or the point where the artist has sold enough recordings to pay back the label for what it has charged in recoupables and begun to collect royalties. If a label has spent $250,000 in recoupables on an artist (basically production and marketing) then the break-even point would be computed by dividing the amount the artist receives for each album sold into the total amount of the recoupables. In this case:

$250,000 divided by $1.05 = 238,095 units or albums

However, if you examine the break-even point from the label's perspective, you will receive a different figure. Here, you would take all the money a label has spent on a project—production costs, other recoupables—and divide that by the wholesale price less the amount for manufacturing and amount paid for mechanicals. In other words, let us suppose a label has spent $250,000 in recoupables. If the album wholesales for $8.30 and it cost $1.25 to manufacture and the mechanicals are $.66 per album, then the cost to the label per album is:

$8.30 - $1.25 - $.66 = $6.39 per album

This would mean that the break-even point for the label would be:

$250,000 divided by $6.39 = 39,124 units

Obviously, there is a rather large gap between 238,095 units and 39,124 units—but that is roughly the gap between the artist's break-even point and the label's break-even point.

Notice that in the label's break-even point, there is no money taken out for royalties; this is because royalties are not paid until the recoupables are earned back. So while an amount might be credited to the artist's account—making the cost per album a bit less in the computations—in reality, it has cost the label *nothing* because this money is set aside on the books—but not actually paid.

The above calculations are an oversimplification of the costs of computing income and expenses on an album. For example, there are additional costs to the American Federation of Musicians (AFM) and the American Federation of Television and Radio Artists (AFTRA) after sales of an album reach a certain plateau; this rewards the creative talent on an album but costs the label additional monies. Also, none of the day-to-day costs of doing business are computed here; there is no provision for rent, salaries, phone bills, and other costs a label must incur in order to conduct business each day. The overhead is high for a label and this break-even point is artificially low and even a bit unfair. But the attempt here is to show the differential between computing costs and profits at a label and how there can be a vast difference between an artist's and a label's break-even point. This also explains how labels can be profitable when 80 percent of their acts are considered "money losers."

Selected Bibliography

Allen, Stanley R. *Audio in Media*. New York: Wadsworth, 1986.

Bagehot, Richard. *Music Business Agreements*. New York: Pergamon, 1989

Baskerville, David. *Music Business Handbook & Career Guide*. Thousand Oaks: Sherwood, 1990.

Brabec, Jeffrey, and Todd Brabec. *Music, Money, and the Recording Artist*. New York: Schirmer, 1994.

Chapple, Steve, and Reebee Garofalo. *Rock'n'Roll Is Here to Pay: The History and Politics of the Music Industry*. Chicago: Nelson-Hall, 1978.

Cramer, Edward M. *In Tune with the Music Business*. New York: Law Arts, 1980.

Csida, Joseph. *The Music/Record Career Handbook*. 2nd ed. New York: Billboard, 1973.

Dearing, James. *Making Money Making Music*. Cincinnati: Writer's Digest, 1990.

Denisoff, R. Serge. *Inside MTV*. New Brunswick, NJ: Transaction, 1991.

—. *Tarnished Gold*. New Brunswick, NJ: Transaction, 1986.

Dranou, Paula. *Inside the Music Publishing Industry*. White Plains, NY: Knowledge, 1980.

Fara, Frank. *How to Open Doors in the Music Industry*. Autumn Gold, 1986.

Field, Shelly. *Career Opportunities in the Music Industry*. New York: Facts on File, 1981.

Fink, Michael. *Inside the Music Business*. New York: Macmillan, 1989.

Frascongna, Xavier M., Jr., and H. Lee Hetherington. *Successful Artist Management: Strategies for Career Development in the Music Industry*. 2nd ed. New York: Billboard, 1990.

Gibson, James. *Getting Noticed: A Musician's Guide to Publicity and Self-Promotion*. Cincinnati: Writer's Digest, 1987.

Halloran, Mark, ed. *The Musicians's Business and Legal Guide*. New Jersey: Prentice-Hall, 1986

Hughes, Barb. *Music Management Made Easy*. Portland: Hughes/Taylor, 1991.

Hurst, Walter E. *How to Be a Music Publisher.* Hollywood, CA: Seven Arts, 1979.

Hurst, Walter E., and William Storm Hale. *Music Record Business and Law: Your Introduction to Music, Record, Copyright, Contracts and Other Business and Law.* Hollywood, CA: Seven Arts, 1974.

——. *Record Industry Book: Stories, Text, Forms, Contracts.* Hollywood, CA: Seven Arts, 1974.

Livingston, Robert Allen. *Livingston's Complete Music Industry Business Reference.* Vols. 1 and 2. Cardiff by the Sea, CA: La Costa Music Business Consultants, 1987.

Martin, George, ed. *Making Music: The Guide to Writing, Performing and Recording.* New York: Morrow, 1983.

Muller, Peter. *Show Business Law.* New York: Quorum, 1991.

Orobko, William. *Musician's Handbook: A Practical Guide to the Law and Business of Music.* Costa Mesa, CA: Self-Counsel Press, 1985.

Passman, Donald. *All You Need to Know About the Music Business.* New York: Simon & Schuster, 1994.

Pettigrew, Jim, Jr. *The Billboard Guide to Music Publicity.* New York: Billboard, 1989.

Rachin, Harvey. *The Encyclopedia of the Music Business.* New York: Harper and Row, 1981.

Rapaport, Diane Sward. *How to Make & Sell Your Own Record: The Complete Guide to Independent Recording.* Jerome, AZ: Jerome Headlands, 1988.

Riordan, James, and Bob Monaco. *Making It in the New Music Business.* Cincinnati: Writer's Digest, 1988.

Riordan, James, and Bob Monaco. *The Platinum Rainbow: How to Succeed in the Music Business Without Selling Your Soul.* Chicago: Contemporary, 1988.

Roth, Ernest. *The Business of Music: Reflections of a Music Publisher.* New York: Oxford UP, 1969.

Sanjek, Russell, and David Sanjek. *American Popular Music Business in the 20th Century.* New York: Oxford UP, 1991.

Shemel, Sidney, and William M. Krasilovsky. *More About This Business of Music.* New York: Billboard, 1989.

——. *This Business of Music.* 6th ed. New York: Billboard, 1990.

Siegel, Alan. *Breaking into the Music Business.* New York: Simon and Schuster, 1990.

Smith, Len Young, et al. *Essentials of Business Law and the Legal Environment.* St. Paul, MN: West, 1992.

Spitz, Robert Stephen. *The Making of a Superstar: Artists and Executives of the Rock Music World*. New York: Anchor, 1978.

Taubman, Joseph. *In Tune with the Music Business*. New York: Law Arts, 1980.

—. *Performing Arts Management and Law*. New York: Law Arts, 1981.

Viera, John David, and Robert Thorne. *Entertainment Publishing and the Arts Handbook*. New York: Clark Boardman, Annually.

Wacholtz, Larry E. *Inside Country Music*. New York: Billboard, 1986.

Wadhams, Wayne. *Sound Advice: The Musician's Guide to the Record Industry*. New York: Schirmer, 1990.

Weissman, Dick. *The Music Business: Career Opportunities and Self-Defense*. New York: Crown, 1990.

Woodhull, Marta. *Singing for a Living*. Cincinnati: Writer's Digest, 1991.

Young, Jean, and Jim Young. *Succeeding in the Big World of Music*. Boston: Little, Brown, 1977.

Zalkind, Ronald. *Getting Ahead in the Music Business*. New York: Schirmer, 1978.

Index

References to subheadings within chapters are in boldface type.

A & R, 41
A & R department and marketing, 41-43
advertising
  print, 109-12
  radio, 106-08
  television, 108-09
  videos, 112-13
advertising department, 28
album cover art, 45-46, 50-52
Alternative Music and Heavy Metal, **126-27**
American Federation of Musicians (AFM), 45, 183
American Federation of Television and Radio Artists (AFTRA), 45, 183
Annie, 137
Appeal, **66-67**
Arbitron, **84**
artist management 36-39
artist royalties 48
Artist's Team, **34-36**
artists
  contract obligation, 43
  and management 31-39
Artwork, **50-52**
ASCAP, 21, 22
Atlantic (label), 165
attributes of great acts, 36
Beatles, 165
Beethoven, 121, 122
Berliner, Emile, 6
Billboard, 86, 87, 88, 163, 165
Bluegrass, **145-46**
Blues, **143-45**
BMG/RCA (label), 13, 117
BMI, 21, 22
booking agents, 24
breakage allowance, 46-47, 178
breaking an act, ten ways of, 31-34
Broadcast Data System, 86
Budgets, **55-58**
bullets, 87
Business Structure and Popular Music, **13-17**
Business Week, 96

Cajun music, 141
Capitol/EMI (label), 13, 117
Caruso, Enrico 7, 121
cassettes, development, 150-51, 152, 154
celebrity concept, 135
Charts, **84-91**
  methodology, 86-88
  random vs. fixed data base, 89-90
Children's Music, **134-38**
  advantages, 135
  Christian, 138

Christian bookstore, 128, 131, 134
Christian music, children's, 138
Christmas, 29
Classical Music, **120-23**
CMT, 113
Columbia (label), 7, 121, 170
comedy recordings, 146-47
compact disc, introduction, 153
concert promoters, 24
Consumers, **96-97**
  contests, 115
  profiles, 12-13
contemporary Christian music, 129-30
contests
  consumer, 115
  in-store, 114-15
Contracts, **43-44**
controlled composition clause, 181
Copyright Act, 23, 181
copyright statutory rate 46
costs
  of a recording label, 173-80
  recoupable and non-recoupable, **44-45**
Country Music, 96
Country Song Round-Up, 96
Crazy Blues, 143
cutouts, 62

dance clubs, role in breaking an act, 33
Dance Music, **125-26**
Davis, Miles, 124
demographics, 84
Direct Mail, **160-61**
Discography, **163-68**
  terms, 165-66
  types of, 166-68
Disneyland, Disneyworld, 137
Distribution, **59-62**
Dolby, Ray, 151
Downbeat, 96
Dylan, Bob, 165

Edison, Thomas, 6, 149, 170
"electronic babysitter," 137
Ethnic Music, **138-41**

Fisher-Price, 137
Folk Music, **141-43**
Forbes, 96
Ford Motor Company, 151
Frets, 96
From Song to Stereo, **25-26**

gifts, music as, 29
Gillespie, Dizzy, 123
Gospel, **127-34**
Grammys, 32, 166
Guitar Player, 96

Harry Fox Agency, 46, 180
heavy metal, 127
Hispanics, 138-40
Holiday, Billie 144
Home Depot, 66
Hopkins, Lightnin', 144
Howlin' Wolf, 144

image, for an artist, 100
independent distributors, 117
independent labels, 117-120
independent promotion, 115-116
Independents, Help From, **115-16**
in-store
  airplay, role in breaking an act, 33
  contests, 114-15
  promotion, 113-15

Jazz, **123-25**
New Age, 124
Jazziz, 96
Johnson, Eldridge, 6

Keyboard, 96
Kid Stuff, 137
Kmart, 11, 60

Latin music, 139-40
Leadbelly, 144
Libraries and Educational Markets, **147**

Mahler, 121
mainstream commercial music, 117
mainstream outlets, 91
Management, for artists, **36-39**
Market Research, **161-63**
data collection methods, 161-62
Marketing, **26-27**
Marketing Music, **17-20**
strategy, 17-20
Marketing Plan, **54-55**
MCA (label), 13, 117
Mechanical Royalties, **46**
mechanicals, 22-23, 181
statutory rate, 181
Media Buys, **106**
Media Layer, **27-28**
MediaPlay, 66
Million Sellers, 166
money flow, in record industry, 21-25
Motorola, 151
movies, role in breaking an act, 33
Mozart, 121, 122
MTV, 31, 113, 156
music and popular culture, 5-7
Music City News, 96
Music in the Market, **10-13**

Nashville Network, 113
National Association of Record Merchandisers (NARM) 166
News Photos, **102-03**

one-stops, 60-61
Other Recoupables or Charge Backs, **47-50**

Packaging, **45-46**
discount, 46, 178
Parker, Charlie "Bird," 123
payola, 116
performance rights organizations, 21-23
personal appearances
for breaking an act, 32
revenue flow, 24-25
Philips, 150
Phonologue, 165
point-of-purchase (POP) material, 44, 47, 50, 51, 113-14, 131
Polygram, 13, 117, 155
popular culture 2, 3, 5, 6, 7, 8, 9, 169, 171
Popular Music in Popular Culture, **7-10**
Presley, Elvis, 165
Press Kits, **95-96**
Press Releases, **101-02**
Price, **59**
Print, **109-12**
print media, for breaking an act, 33
Problems with the Charts, **89-91**
Producer's Royalties, **47**
Production Costs, **45**
Programming, radio, **80-82**
promoters, concert, 24

promotion, record
  independent, 77-78, 115-16
  in-store, 113-115
  and publicity, 97
  radio, 28, 73, 74, 76
  six steps of, 73-74
Promotion Network, **74-78**
publicists, role of, 93, 94
publicity
  bio, 99-100
  department , 28
  photos, 51-52, 102-04
  press kits, 99-100, 103-05
  press releases, 101-02
  strategy, 94-95
  tools of, 99-100
  tour, 96, 105-06
Publicity and Promotion, **98**
Publicity Plan, **97**
publishing revenue, 22-24

rack jobbers, 60
Radio, **78-84, 106-08**
  advertising 106-08
  for breaking an act, 31
  Christian 132
  college, 120, 122, 143, 144
  gospel, 130
  primary function, 78
  promotion, 28
  public, 120, 122, 142, 144
  and record industry, 78-79
  and record labels, 73-74
  reporting stations, 75
  shifts, 79
  Spanish-language, 140
Radio and Records (R&R), 87
Radio Programming, **82-83**
Rainey, Ma, 144
Rap music, **126,** 142
rating formula, 84
Ratings and Shares, **79-80**
RCA, 121, 149, 165
Record Company, 10, **69-71**
  contract obligation, 43
  income, 11
  relations with retailers, 69-71
record stores
  appeal, 66-67
  types of, 63-66
Recording Industry Association of
  America (RIAA), 166
recoupable expenses, 44, 177
Retailer's Perspective, **67-69**
retailers and record companies,
  63-66
returns, 62
revenue streams, 25
Royalty Base Rate, **46-47**

Scheduling, **52-54**
SESAC, 21
share formula, 84
small businesses, 14-17
Smith, Bessie, 144
Smith, Mamie, 143
Sony (label), 13, 117, 155
SoundScan, 22, 88, 163
Spanish-language radio, 140
Special Marketing, **157-60**
specialty music, 118
Spoken Word Recordings, **146-47**
Strategy (publicity), **94-95**

Target 11, 60
technology in marketing, 149-57
Television, **108-09**
  advertising, 108-09
  for breaking an act, 32
  Christian, 132
  marketing, 157-60
  public, 142

theater, for breaking an act, 32-33
Time 33, 96
Tools of Publicity: The Bio, **99-100**
Tour Publicity, **104-05**

Victor Records, 6, 7, 121, 170
video, kids, 137
videos, 112-13
    for breaking an act, 31-32

Wal-Mart, 11, 60, 61
Walt Disney, 136
Warner Brothers, 162
Waters, Muddy, 144
WEA, 13, 117
Whitburn, Joel, 165
Why People Buy Recordings, **28-30**